BOOK OF THE
MIXED BREED DOG

The Authors

Kay White, MIACE, writes regularly for many canine magazines, including the *Veterinary Times, Kennel Gazette,* and *Dog World*. She has written and co-written fourteen books about dogs and cats, and has pioneered the provision of educational facilities for dog owners and breeders. She attends and reports on the major veterinary conferences and meetings on animal behavior, and used to own boarding and breeding kennels in Surrey, England. Kay White now lives in Sussex with her husband and four dogs.

Andrew Prentis BVSc, MRCVS, is Director of the Beaumont Animals' Hospital, a teaching hospital of the Royal Veterinary College in London. He has also worked as Veterinary Technical Director of the Society for the Protection of Animals in North Africa, and from 1986–1991 he was Veterinary Director of the RSPCA's Southern Hospital Group.

BOOK OF THE
MIXED BREED
DOG

KAY WHITE MIACE
HEALTH CARE: ANDREW PRENTIS BVSC, MRCVS

Originally published in English by
HarperCollins*Publishers* Ltd under the title:
RSPCA BOOK OF THE MONGREL
© HarperCollins*Publishers* Ltd, 1997

Kay White asserts the moral right to be identified as
the author of this work.

American text edited by Joe Stahlkuppe, Mt. Olive, AL

First edition for the United States, Canada, and the
Philippine Republic published by Barron's Educational
Series, Inc., 1998

Copyright © 1998 U.S. version, Barron's Educational
Series, Inc.

All inquiries should be addressed to:
Barron's Educational Series, Inc.
250 Wireless Boulevard, Hauppauge, New York 11788

Library of Congress Catalog Card No. 97-26737
International Standard Book No. 0-7641-5065-0

Library of Congress Cataloging-in-Publication Data

White, Kay.
  [Book of the mongrel]
  Book of the mixed breed dog / Kay White, Andrew Prentis.
     p.   cm.
  Originally published: Book of the mongrel. London : HarperCollins, 1997.
  Includes index.
  ISBN 0-7641-5065-0
  1. Mutts (Dogs)   I. Prentis, Andrew.   II. Title.
SF427.W415   1998
636.7—dc21   97-26737
                                                    CIP

This book was created by SP Creative Design for HarperCollins*Publishers* Ltd
Photography by David Dalton and Rolando Ugolini
Editor: Heather Thomas
Design and production: Rolando Ugolini
Artwork: Al Rockal and Rolando Ugolini

Color reproduction by Colourscan, Singapore

Printed and bound by New Interlitho, SpA, Milan, Italy

9 8 7 6 5 4 3 2 1

CONTENTS

FOREWORD

At some point in the history of their development, every breed of dog was first mixed bred, and only over a long period of time did they become purebred. There is a wonderful sense of aesthetic and behavioral predictability to many of the purebred dogs, but the mixed breeds, too, have special qualities. They have a level of bonding and interaction along with what is known to scientists as hybrid vigor. These qualities are as important and as bright and shining in the wonderful world of pet owning as the predictability factor of purebred dogs.

In brief, there really is no choice between purebred and mixed breed dogs that can be dictated from the outside—it is a matter of personal taste and one's heart. Personally, I have always felt that the ideal home contained both purebred and mixed breeds, preferably animals rescued from shelters and pounds. They make the finest aesthetic mix of all—as long as breeding is impossible.

However you view it, purebred or mixed breed, they all are, in the final analysis, pure because they are all dog. For tens of thousands of years they have been pure dog with no kangaroo, no giraffe, no canary or lion mixed in. What can be purer than that—pure dog?

Roger Caras
The American Society for the Prevention of Cruelty to Animals

WHAT ARE MIXED BREED DOGS?

L et's begin by saying that it's not an insult to call a dog a mixed breed, or even a mongrel. The word mongrel is derived from the now obsolete Middle English word *Meng* (to mix) or the Old English *Gemong* (a mingling). A mixed breed dog is a combination of breeds, in contrast with what we term pedigree dogs, which may have been bred selectively for thousands of years, whether or not the parents had a recorded pedigree.

Early Egyptian paintings of dogs, *circa* 4,000 B.C., show hounds not unlike the Greyhounds and Whippets that we know today. These early dogs, which are thought to be domesticated individuals from the smaller wolf strains, had no written pedigree, but they were bred like to like in looks and in speed and hunting ability, that is, they were selected for and developed to use their natural attributes for the benefit of man. At the other end of the ancient canine size scale is the Pekingese, known and treasured as "under the table dogs" by the emperor and the court of the Han dynasty in China, around 200 B.C. Pekingese were not working dogs; on the contrary, they were kept solely for the pleasure they gave and as objects of beauty.

As the early nomadic tribes settled and engaged in agricultural work as a way of life, dogs that could herd livestock and also guard them from wolves and other predators became important. In Britain in the Middle Ages, dogs were a very important part of the sporting passions of the day: bull-baiting and stag hunting.

SELECTIVE BREEDING

Dogs have been selectively bred down the ages to hunt game, to chase and catch, to retrieve, to scent, to go after vermin, and also to guard man and his property against intruders.

Each type of dog was developed with the physique and physical conformation best suited to his appointed work. A dog's speed and willingness to work was an attribute for the owner to boast about and, consequently, family lines of dogs

Above: Mixed breed dogs with terrier ancestry may have shaggy or wiry coats and a strong independent streak.

that had a standard of excellence were in demand. From these family lines, the concept of recorded pedigrees developed but this was many years after recognizable breeds of dogs were known and used. For example, English Foxhound pedigree recording began in 1787.

However, if you should ever be made to feel that your dog lacks a pedigree written down for all to see, perhaps it may be a comfort to remember that there is no positive proof to link any dog to its recorded pedigree. And if you want to boast about the antiquity of your own dog's line, you may be interested to know that one of the oldest dog skeletons found in Britain, at Avebury in Wiltshire, and thought to date from before 3,000 B.C., was a domestic dog of unidentified breed. It was long-legged, short-backed, and small-headed with a skull shorter than that of a hound. Therefore it was not a specialized dog, and not intended for hunting, herding, or guarding—just a dog, which archaeologists identified as a kind of ancient British pariah dog.

The word "pariah" is an Indian one, and is applied to feral dogs that live in and around villages but that are not owned by any one person. These dogs generally scavenge for food and live on the fringes of society. Although they have neither territory nor possessions to protect, they do not necessarily welcome human contact.

As the writer Hugh Walpole described his own dog in the *Jeremy and Hamlet* stories written in the 1930s:

"I have owned a great many dogs, some of them very finely bred, very aristocratic, very intelligent but none of them has ever approached Hamlet for wisdom, conceit, self-reliance and true affection.

He was a ghastly mongrel, I tremble to think of the many different breeds of dogs that have gone into his making, but he had Character, he had Heart, he had an unconquerable zest for life."

Does that not sum up all the mixed breeds we know?

CASUALLY BRED DOGS

Mixed breeds are truly bred at whim, hardly ever asking their owner's permission for the coupling and rarely requiring any persuasion to mate as some of the more inhibited pedigree breeds do. These dogs may well be the product of many generations of chance matings; no wonder some people call them "Heinz 57s," reflecting the famous advertisements for that company's fifty-seven product lines. Others call them "curs" but this is an unkind term, originally referring to a vicious mongrel, and shortened from the thirteenth-century word *Kurdogge* and the old Norse word for "growl." Another term, which has fallen into disuse, is the Yorkshire expression, a "tyke," meaning a rough-coated, shaggy mixed breed. Some people call mixed dogs "mutts" but that word has overtones of stupidity and mixed dogs are usually very bright, quick to learn, and as easy to train as any purebred dog.

Nearly everyone likes to speculate on the breeds that created their own mixed breed dog, but in fact this is only really possible in crossbreeds. True mixed breeds have more ingredients than a Christmas fruitcake and it is almost impossible to know which of their assortment of genes will dominate their looks. They have infinite and unpredictable variety. Even when two similar mixed breeds are mated together, it is very possible that none of the offspring will resemble in color and markings either of their parents.

The genes of mixed dogs are like the pretty pieces of glass in a kaleidoscope; if you shake them up, then a different design is likely to result every time.

SIZE

One of the frequently quoted drawbacks in taking on a mixed puppy is that you can't predict how big he will grow, but true mixed breeds are rarely extreme in size. They are most frequently average in size, with a height range of between 15–16 in. (38–41 cm) minimum and 22–23 in. (54–57 cm) maximum.

However, it is important that we learn to differentiate between mixed breeds and crossbreeds. A crossbreed results from the mating of two purebred dogs of different breeds. For example, little dogs, such as Yorkshire Terriers and Papillons, are sometimes mated together, and these crossbreeds are likely to be small.

THE LOOK OF MIXED BREED DOGS

Mixed breed dogs are generally medium size and their muzzles are often pointed. The broad-muzzled, flat-faced type of dog, as seen in Boxers and Pugs, rarely survives even the first crossing.

◆ **Ears** may be pricked up, and open, ready to catch every sound; or they may be folded over or set on the side of the face and hanging down; or the dog may have one of each kind. The ears may be set high on the head, or down at eye level. On-top ears are the most flexible kind: one or both may be cocked up to demonstrate their alertness, or they may be flexed backward and flattened to indicate fear or apprehension. Some ears may be fringed and drooping, sometimes with an attractive hairdresser-style flick-up at the tips. One ear held higher than the other may indicate a painful ear problem, or it may be just the way your dog likes to carry them. The great thing about mixed breed dogs is that they and their owners see no reason to conform to any preconceived designs.

◆ **Tails** have infinite variety too. They may be wonderfully plumed and feathered and curled over the back like a teapot handle, or held out behind like a fox's brush. On a smooth-coated mixed breed the tail also may be smooth and thick like a mooring rope, held aloft like a signaling flag or carried down as a rudder. But, just for fun, a smooth-coated dog may sport a feathered plume.

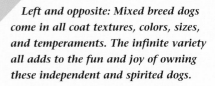

Left and opposite: Mixed breed dogs come in all coat textures, colors, sizes, and temperaments. The infinite variety all adds to the fun and joy of owning these independent and spirited dogs.

DOCKING

There is never any case for trying to get a mixed breed's or a crossbreed's tail docked. The tail is a very important communication aid, especially when indicating their friendly intentions to other dogs, so never attempt to deprive the dog of this valuable and vital asset.

◆ **Coats** can be of any texture, quite smooth with densely packed short hairs, or with slightly longer and silky hair, or long and shaggy all over, about 5–6 in. (12.5–15 cm) long. Some dogs have stiff wire hair and bristly whiskers on the muzzle. Dense wire-haired coats may need professional stripping at least once a year, and your pet will appreciate having the dead hair removed, and he will look better.

◆ **Eyes** may be round or oval: the color range is from bluish gray, through amber and yellow to very dark brown.

◆ **The nose** of a mixed breed dog will be related to its coat pigment. Mixed breeds usually don't undergo the pinkish and grayish seasonal change in nose color that affects some pedigree breeds.

◆ **Coat color** is another rainbow story. Tans, brown, black with tan trimmings, all over golden or foxy red, white with black patches, black with white shirtfront, black with white ticking, white with red saddle and ears, white with irregular red or brown patches, each in its own way attractive. More unusual is the brindle effect

coat, set off by touches of white. The most commonly seen mixed breed wears a medium-length solid black or black and tan coat grown at random length, sometimes accompanied by a smart white shirtfront, but these dogs are often passed over when people go to choose a pet from an animal shelter.

Above: This mischievous little dog has clearly identifiable Westie ancestry.

◆ Mixed breeds that live in considerate, kind homes and have been adopted early in their lives are often of middle-weight athletic build with straight front legs and well-muscled hind legs especially suited to high jumping. Dogs that have had a hard time in their youth may never quite achieve the hard, conditioned body and luxuriant coat that they might have had.

◆ The mixed breed's talent shows through in the way in which they recover their trust in humans even when they have endured very bad treatment, which they have done nothing to deserve.

Left: Many mixed breeds are fun-loving and intelligent dogs who need a lot of stimulating games and exercise.

CROSSBREEDS

Crossbreeds are the result of mating two different pure breeds together. Such matings may arise by accident, when two different breeds are kept in one household or in one kennel compound. Occasionally, a crossbreeding is deliberately undertaken in order to introduce features lacking in a purebred dog. Although it is not a common practice today, crossbreeding has been done by dog breeders and others for the betterment of a particular breed. The deliberate production of crossbred puppies, especially by someone other than a real expert, should be avoided. Dog breeding involves a large number of genetic variables, even within dogs of the same breed. These variables are greatly increased when two or

Below: This Border Collie crossbred dog may be the result of a deliberate or accidental mating.

Left: German Shepherd influence is clearly evident in this dog's head shape and ear carriage.

more breeds are mixed together.

Dogs that aren't of sufficient quality for the breeding of top-quality purebred dogs should always be spayed or neutered. This certainly includes all mixed dogs.

Scott and Fuller, the geneticists and animal behaviorists who studied a dog population in an American experimental laboratory in 1965, mated together Basenjis and Cocker Spaniels. The resultant litter was unlike either of the parents, but when the pups were, in time, backcrossed to a Cocker, or to a Basenji, traces of the ancestral features were shown.

The most famous crossbreds of our time are probably Queen Elizabeth's Dorgis, an accidental litter resulting from a mating between a Dachshund and a Corgi. A painting of the queen surrounded by her Corgis and a Dorgi hangs in The U.K. Kennel Club, casting a bright eye over all the purebreds registered there.

IDENTIFYING ANCESTRY

Crossbred ancestry in the first generation of the cross can be picked out fairly easily: German Shepherd dog influence comes through very strongly in head shape and ear carriage; English Springer Spaniels pass

GUIDE DOGS

The Guide Dogs for the Blind Association in Britain have created one of the most useful crosses in mating Labradors to Golden Retrievers, to attempt to blend the best attributes of both breeds. The resulting litters have proved to have an extremely high success rate as dogs for guiding blind people: the willingness to cooperate with the owner, shown by the Labrador, has blended well with the instinctive liveliness and agility of the Golden Retriever. However, this cross is made once only, and the crossbreds are not bred back to each other, as guide dogs are spayed or neutered.

KENNEL CLUB REGISTRATION

The American Kennel Club regulations about registration state that no dog shall be entered on any breed register unless each of its parents is entered in that register. Imported dogs of new breeds go onto a special register, but only if they have come from a country where there is a recognized kennel club. The American Kennel Club only allows purebred dogs to compete in conformation shows and performance events, with the exception of Canine Good Citizen tests. The United Kennel Club allows mixed breed dogs in some performance events. Dogs of mixed breeding can be great in many events; it is only that their opportunities are more limited than those of purebred dogs.

on their coloring and markings, as do Border Collies. Black coloring will often dominate all other colors. Mixing dogs that have a very distinctive coat can bring about problems later in life: for instance, a Labrador crossed with an Old English Sheepdog may retain the Labrador's double undercoat but may grow a long Old English Sheepdog coat on top of it. The shedding problems and the overheating may create their own difficulties for the owner.

Character traits may not blend well either—a cross between a Doberman Pinscher and a Jack Russell Terrier may create an aggressive dog whose bite may well be as bad as his bark. The keep-on-running attributes of a Saluki, crossed with the riot-raising potential of a Border Collie, may also not make an easy-to-live-with dog. A cross that appears to be most successful is that of a Yorkshire Terrier with a Maltese Terrier. These dogs may be larger than the average Yorkie, but sport a "bad

hair day" kind of coat of a rough texture in silver and gold coloring.

When writing of crossbreeds, it may be useful to point out that if a pedigree bitch has a litter by a dog that is not of her own breed, there is no truth in the belief that all future litters will be tainted in some way. Mated to an individual in her own

JACK RUSSELLS

These very popular little terriers make lively and interesting pets. Their coloring is mainly white with tan or red patches, and the coat may be wirehaired or smooth, both varieties thereby betraying their Fox Terrier ancestry.

Jack Russell Terriers are quite popular in the United States. The television show *Frasier* has the canine character Eddie, a Jack Russell, in the cast. Jack Russells still show a lot of breed variation with some crossbred or mixed breed dogs being passed off as pure JRTs.

This terrier is reminiscent of the type said to have been bred in the early nineteenth century by the Reverend John Russell, after whom the breed is named.

breed, the bitch will have a purebred litter which can be registered with a kennel club. But to breed a crossbred to another crossbred is to lose many of the original attributes and those who do so are creating a mixed breed dog.

HEALTH

Mixed breed dogs are popularly supposed to be healthier than purebred dogs, and this may well be true, given that the close inbreeding of some pedigree dogs tends to concentrate the genes that produce hereditary diseases, such as hip dysplasia, some heart defects, abnormalities of the eyes, and skin problems. Not every purebred dog suffers from these diseases, but a considerable number do.

However, mixed breed dogs do not carry such an intensity of inherited characteristics, although they are just as susceptible to all the infectious diseases, such as distemper and its complications, leptospirosis, hepatitis, canine parvovirus, and infectious tracheobronchitis, familiarly known as kennel cough. Mixed breeds are just as susceptible to internal and external parasites, to digestive problems and chronic diarrhea, to kidney problems, obstructions of the throat and gut, and food poisoning through scavenging. So mixed breeds are by no means exempt from veterinary expenses.

Crossbreeds, unless intentionally and carefully planned, may come with

Above: A terrier mix showing its willingness to retrieve.

the hereditary diseases of both their parents, and those further back in their pedigree. Dogs of mixed breeding may be quite healthy, but can also inherit disabilities and health conditions from their parents.

TEMPERAMENT AND ATTRIBUTES

Many fans of mixed breeds will agree that no matter what their dog's ancestry, he has inherited agility, cleverness, and the ability to learn quickly and to continue to apply what he has learned, plus abundant vigor to join in whatever his human family wants to do.

ANTISOCIAL BEHAVIOR

Possibly the worst trait that any dog can inherit is a passion for running free, for wandering, and for scavenging. Although mixed breed dogs have a reputation for roaming, they are no more likely to do so than purebred dogs. However difficult it may seem, all dogs must be confined within their owner's premises. Community leash laws require that they may not roam free. Among the worst habits of free-roaming dogs is that of hanging around outside houses where bitches in season are kept, and molesting them when they are out for walks with their owners. This trait is not actually the dogs' fault, but is caused by the irresponsible behavior of dog owners. Certainly any unneutered male shows no hesitation in running and creating problems, but it is the owner who ultimately should be in control of the dog.

It is not justifiable to say that a free-running dog has a charming temperament and means no harm when he teases the Rottweiler walking sedately on the lead or when he jumps playfully around the elderly woman who is concerned about her shopping.

Free-running dogs, whether purebred or mixed, are not socially acceptable. Dogs can appear to be very clever at crossing the road in perfect safety but they do not always get it right, and some

Below: It is important for dogs to socialize and to meet other dogs, even when on the lead, without behaving aggressively toward each other.

ANTI-DOG LEGISLATION

There are many locales in the United States that have passed or may pass laws and ordinances against certain breeds or types of dogs. These laws have come about because some owners of certain kinds of dogs have been irresponsible. Dog bite cases have become commonplace and have resulted not only in painful, often scarring injuries, but some fatalities, especially among children.

The very existence of so many mixed breed dogs is ample evidence that many dog owners have been unable or unwilling to keep their pets at home. It is also true that many dog owners have not faced their

responsibilities in having their pets either spayed or neutered. These simple yet inexpensive operations will play a large part in stopping the overwhelming canine population in the United States.

Before anyone chooses to allow a litter of puppies to be born, pure breed or mixed breed, a visit should be made to an animal shelter to see the large number of dogs and puppies in need of homes.

A further reality must also be understood. Many or most of these pet wanna-bes will be killed because there are simply more dogs than there are homes for them.

dogs sustain terrible, often fatal, injuries just because their owners let them run free. Worse still, some multiple-vehicle crashes occur because a car swerves to avoid a dog that is running in the road.

If you take pleasure in owning a mixed breed dog, then he must be cared for in just the same way as an expensive pedigree dog. He must not be allowed to chase cars and bicycles, overturn trash cans, bark intolerably, leave feces on the pavement, pick fights with other dogs, or run loose in children's playgrounds.

Mixed breed dogs must be protected from behaving badly just as vigilantly as the rarest of pedigree specimens. There is

no place for badly behaved and antisocial dogs in modern society.

CONTROL

Some feel that the desire to run free, to perform daring feats of athletic behavior by jumping into a neighbor's yard, to dash across streets and to track down every bitch in the neighborhood is buried deeply in the subconscious of every dog.

Dogs used to be tolerated in urban and suburban streets. In earlier times, the streets were often full of dogs. Control of stray and abandoned dogs today depends not on the American Kennel Club, the dog show community, or on those persons who responsibly breed purebred dogs. The average pet owner must shoulder the guilt for the number of dogs that run free.

Dog owners who neglect their pets and allow them free-range in cities or rural areas are part of a major problem. This problem costs many millions of dollars each year. There is no reckoning of the costs in accidents, dog bites, injuries, and loss of property also associated with the ecology of the free-ranging dog.

In cities, dogs are seen scavenging through dumps and trash cans. They contribute to automobile accidents and spread parasites and disease. The life expectancy for these dogs is meted out in days rather than in months and years.

Stray dogs reproduce with alarming success. Their fertility is not only part of the stray dog's existence, but stray males can jump fences and impregnate stay-at-home females. In either scenario, another unwanted litter of puppies is born.

Stray dogs in rural areas can become both scavengers and predators—preying not only on wild animals but also on domestic livestock. These strays are sometimes abandoned pets whose owners felt that, irrationally, they would fare better outdoors than by being turned over to their local shelter. Animal shelters have been besieged by the numbers of former pets that have become strays. Tax dollars and donations go to maintain these shelters, but more and more homeless animals have stretched many of these facilities beyond their capacities. Only through a change in the mind-set of the American dog-owning public can this canine avalanche be contained.

Left: Your dog should always be under control. When taking him out for a walk in a public place, put him on a lead.

DECIDING TO ACQUIRE A DOG

You and your family have probably had the same discussion over and over again. You all want a dog, and you have decided you want the pleasure and reward of owning a mixed breed or crossbreed. However, before making an irrevocable decision, you have to take a long, honest look at yourself, your immediate family, your lifestyle, and your future prospects. "A Dog is for Life," as the slogan goes, so if you do take on a dog you will be putting yourself, or someone close to you, into the role of a canine foster parent for at least the next ten years. Can you foresee that you will be able to give a dog all that he needs for that time? What if your own life changes? Are you sure there will always be a suitable home, human companionship, and affectionate care for the dog for that length of time?

The promise you make when you decide to have a dog or a puppy is increasingly difficult to keep when very few people are able to forecast their future income, job, and homes; so the very

best you can do is to say that wherever you go, your dog will go too. Your home, accommodations, and leisure pursuits will also always be chosen with the dog in mind. You cannot divorce your dog; their devotion to their owner is too strong for that. It is true that if you take a puppy or a grown dog from an animal shelter, you

assume the role of a fosterowner, and the shelter may promise to take the dog back if you cannot keep him. But this is no way to treat a dog: to take him into your home when it suits you and to send him back when he becomes inconvenient. Could you bear to see your dog put back into a compartment in a communal kennel, to wait day after day hoping that you will come through the door to claim him again—that the banishment has all been a dreadful mistake?

Once you have bonded with the dog and made him yours, that is what he is—your dog. You are considering adopting a living creature that will become part of your family, in sickness and in health, in fun and frolics, in deliberate naughtiness and in incredible cleverness, in joy and laughter, and in much appreciated comforting companionship.

Right: Having enough time to spend with a pet is a crucial factor in deciding to own a dog.

COMPANIONSHIP

Puppies and grown dogs have so much to give us, but what they need is our companionship in return. True, you need space for a dog, and you need money for his feeding, training, and health care, but most of all you need time. There is no purebred dog, mixed breed, or crossbreed who enjoys or even tolerates being left alone for long periods of time.

We have to remember that dogs, and the wolves who were their ancestors,

originally lived in packs. Members of the pack are playmates, disciplinarians, decision makers, comforters, and teachers for each other. A good attentive owner can fulfill all these roles, but the dog left on his own is a sorry creature; dogs feel loneliness more than any other pets.

Puppies under six months of age need someone home with them for most of the day. Dogs over six months can be alone for the average workday but when bringing a bewildered new puppy into the home, a responsible adult should plan to take several days off to help him settle in and begin a successful adjustment to life with a new family. When a pet has to be left at home during the workday, every consideration is made to keep the homebound canine safe and comfortable. If you must leave your pet outside, provide a secure (and fenced) backyard with a weatherproof doghouse.

Dogs are not unlike children. They can be a nuisance at times, and they can curtail our freedom to do exactly as we wish—to come home or to stay away just as the whim takes us. "I've got to get back to the dog" sounds a bit foolish to non-dog owners, but it is true; you have a duty to your animal to fulfill.

HOME ALONE
When you take on a dog, your house and yard are bound to suffer some damage, and at times your dog may be a defiant

SHOULD YOU HAVE A DOG?

◆ Are you allowed to have a dog where you live now? A surprising number of desirable homes do not allow dogs; inquire first rather than argue later.

◆ You have to consider your leisure time. Do you do things on weekends that will allow the dog to join in? For example, sailing and cycling are not dog-friendly activities unlike walking and dog-orientated training and agility games.

◆ Dog ownership should be viewed as a privilege with responsibilities. Many people who can't or shouldn't own a dog due to their lifestyles and other constraints can find fulfillment in volunteering at animal shelters, visiting dog shows, and caring for the pets of friends and neighbors. You don't always have to own a dog to enjoy a dog!

disobeyer of your rules of conduct. Some dogs are harder to fence in than others. Make every effort to make sure that your pet is safe and comfortable—at home!

The problem of stray and homeless dogs in past decades has given rise to an aggressive anti-dog mentality in some places. Animal control officers, the dog catchers of former years, are much more vigorous in their activities. A dog owner

ADULT DOG OR PUPPY?

Do you want an adult dog or a puppy? If you have the time to look after him, a pup might be the best choice. However, if you already have a dog in your household, a grown dog may be resentful of another adult being brought in. Most dogs will accept and enjoy a puppy. Your adult may help you in training the puppy in house manners and being a comforter to him in the lonely hours of the night.

now must realize that his or her right to own a pet ends at the boundaries of other people's rights to be free from problems caused by a neighborhood dog.

LONELINESS

Loneliness is the one most constant factor that breaks down the dog/human relationship. Some people end up disliking their dogs if they tear up the house or soil the floors every time they go out. However, you should never forget that you may be the cause of these behavior patterns. If you leave the dog alone for long periods of time, you are expecting too much from a very intelligent animal that was not

created for a solitary existence. This is especially true if you take an adult dog from an animal shelter, as being alone will be totally alien to his experience. In kennels there are other dogs in neighboring pens, there are always kennel workers about and there are even visitors to bring a social atmosphere. It is doubtful that any dog visualizes a real home as a custom-built kitchen into which he is shut alone all day.

What every dog requires from you is companionship and, a measure of patience. You should always be concerned about your dog's safety and comfort. This includes daily attention, care, and affection. Dogs are truly companion animals and they need their owners to guide them.

MAINTENANCE COSTS

What about costs? Apart from the initial purchase price, the maintenance costs of a mixed breed are about the same as those for a pedigree dog of the same size.

◆ **FEEDING**

We have come a long way from the time when it was customary to feed a pet dog on household scraps. We know now that to keep a dog in good health, he must have a balanced diet of carbohydrates, protein, fat, vitamins, and minerals.

Most people rely on a good brand of dry or canned dog food.

◆ The right amount of food for your dog depends on the choice of food, the size and age of your pet, and the animal's activity level. Follow the directions on the can or bag of food, and increase or decrease portions based on the dog's weight. Many nutritionists believe that good quality dry kibbles provide a dog with complete nutrition and that canned food need not be fed.

◆ Puppies cost more to feed in their first year while they are growing. It should be possible to work out, from studying the prices of the dog foods on the supermarket shelves, the basic costs of feeding the dog you hope to have.

◆ **HEALTH COSTS**

Other necessary expenses will be veterinarian's fees for unexpected major illnesses and injuries; and veterinary fees for regular needs, such as vaccinations,

worming, and anti-flea treatments.

◆ **EQUIPMENT**

You will also need to purchase some basic items of dog equipment, such as a folding cage or crate, grooming tools, chew toys, collars and leads, a bed, food and water bowls, and a dog tag bearing your name, address and phone number.

◆ **BOARDING FEES**

If you go away on vacation and cannot take your dog with you, you may also have to pay boarding kennel fees or hire a pet sitter for your dog.

DO SOME RESEARCH

As a prospective first-time dog owner, you should look around at your dog-owning friends, and at the local dogs in the park—and at the many dogs and puppies available at shelters. Doubtless you will soon come to the conclusion that it would be lovely to have the constant companionship of a dog, and you will be absolutely right. But there is also a down side. Your dog will need

Below: Many dogs regard their crates as safe havens and dens, but don't leave a puppy or young dog locked in its cage or crate if you leave home for the entire day.

companionship from you, and, at times, that may be inconvenient and will curb your own freedom. Puppies and adult dogs acquired from a rescue society or animal shelter will require a great deal of patience from you, the owner. Someone responsible must be there with the dog and for the dog.

Puppies and dogs cannot train themselves; they need a sensible human on hand to teach them. If you take an adult dog from a shelter, he may well need as much house and behavior training as a puppy. You may have to begin all over again when a dog has spent some time in kennels and got used to a way of life where a consistent relief schedule is not part of the normal routine.

Kenneled dogs may bark constantly and cause complaints from your neighbors; and dogs put out in garages and runs are not learning in-house behavior, nor are they any deterrent to intruders.

DAYTIME SOLUTIONS
There are ways in which a working owner can manage to keep a dog, but having

someone "pop in at lunchtime" is not a fail-safe solution for young pups. The "popping in" time is all too short, and is mostly spent on clearing up what a puppy has done in a four-hour morning.

Crates and cages can be used in a laundry room, kitchen, or bathroom, when a puppy or adult dog must be left for the entire day. The section of the floor of this dog-safe room should be covered with newspapers and ample drinking water should be provided.

The advantage of the wire crate is that the dog can see all that is happening, can be spoken to by passing humans, and the wire door can be left open or closed as suits the situation. Dogs love their crates; they act as a den and a safe place in which to sleep and eat. The crates may seem expensive as an initial purchase, but in so many ways they are an invaluable aid to dog living, and much kinder, both at home and when traveling, than shutting a dog away completely. However, an adult dog should never be shut into a crate when he is alone in the house for more than nine to ten hours.

LIVING ACCOMMODATION AND EXERCISE SPACE

Many people find that they are able to keep a pet dog quite successfully while living in an apartment. Modified housebreaking, perhaps in the form of paper training, must be used when

WORKING AT HOME

People who can work from home are ideally suited to have a dog, but it should be pointed out that the three- to nine-month-old puppy stage can be very disruptive to a planned work schedule. However, your puppy will be house-trained all the quicker, and a little play in the yard is a great break for both dog and owner.

apartment dwellers can't get their puppies outside quickly to defecate and urinate. Regular walks are a necessity to keep the dog well exercised and well socialized. Walk your dog at least three times a day.

Knowing when your pup eats and how much it eats is crucial to timing outside visits. Planning for relief trips is also a key part of the scheduling that is necessary for any urban dweller.

THE BACKYARD

Suburban and rural dog owners may have more options because of the availability of fenced backyards. Yards, however, don't take away all of the owner's responsibilities. Yards must always be fenced and appropriately so to the size of the dog. Large dogs can clear fences of 5 and 6 feet (1.5 and 1.8 m) in height with great ease. Smaller dogs, especially terrier types, can dig out from under.

Above: Train your puppy to walk on a lead from the earliest possible age.

Because most pet owners will want to share their homes with their pooches, it is necessary for all dogs to be house-broken, even if a large fenced backyard is available. Designate a special spot in the yard as the "relief area." When taking the dog outside for a urination or defecation break, go directly to this spot. Wait until the pet has finished, then praise him enthusiastically, thereby reinforcing that the dog has done what it was supposed to do where it was supposed to do it.

Always be certain that the yard is safe for the dog. Some yard plants, like daffodils, can be poisonous. Items in the backyard may fall on and injure (or kill) an inquisitive pet. Don't just put a dog or puppy in the yard and go off and forget about it. Fresh water must always be available and so should shelter in the form of a good doghouse for those times when being outside is best for the pet.

EXERCISE AREAS

Where would you take your dog for a good run off the lead? Is there a safely fenced park where dogs can run free nearby? Suitable places are becoming more difficult to find; many parks and beaches are forbidden to dogs, even when accompanied by their owners. Your dog must be completely under your control before you can contemplate letting him off the lead. A dog off-leash is always a risk. He could be distracted by a squirrel, a bicyclist, or a jogger and not heed your call. Practice the "come when called" routine (see page 74), giving lots of praise and a food reward when the dog comes instantly back to you.

Walking your dog off the lead in a town street or along a busy road is purely exhibitionism on the owner's part. There will always be some overwhelming distraction, which will cause the dog to disobey and run across the road. You also have to consider other walkers, who may feel reluctant to pass a dog that is not

FEAR AND DISLIKE OF DOGS

Dog owners must realize that not everybody gets the same pleasure out of being around dogs that they do. Some people are fearful of dogs, and although we know that Ol' Rover wouldn't hurt a flea, they don't know that. Responsible dog ownership means not causing difficulties for others. Do this by always keeping your dog under control, not going into someone else's "space" with a dog without being invited, and being alert to situations where a dog can get into trouble. Be considerate of other people. They have the same right to dislike dogs that you have to like them. You wouldn't want their anti-dog sentiments to affect you—don't let your pro-dog feelings affect them.

under full control. Extending leads are not the answer, can be dangerous, and should only be used in unfenced open areas. You may feel you are giving your dog a measure of freedom by having him on the full extent of a long lead, but he could ensnare other walkers by wrapping the lead around their legs.

You, as the owner, are liable for the damage your dog does to other people or their possessions. You should always avoid potential litigation by being a responsible dog owner. Control your pet with safe shelter, appropriate fencing, strong leashes and collars, and good obedience training. You may also want to increase your homeowner's insurance to handle any situations at home that you can't avoid. This is where your dog's insurance policy comes to your aid. Most policies, which are taken out primarily for covering veterinary fees, also carry substantial Third Party Cover.

YOUR OWN LIFESTYLE

Before you obtain a dog, you should make a clear assessment of your personal lifestyle. Are the things that you do conducive to adding a dog to them?

Your new dog may force you to make some hard decisions about the things you want to do with your leisure time. Spending time with your dog is an excellent leisure time activity. Perhaps this pooch can replace some activities and even bring others into your life. There will always be regular and unexpected expenses attached to becoming a dog owner, even of a mixed breed dog. If your lifestyle and standard of living doesn't allow you enough extra money to properly feed, shelter, and care for a dog, you should postpone dog ownership until you can afford it. Don't get a dog if you can't fit it easily into your busy schedule. A dog relegated to possession status is a sorry sight indeed. Dogs long to be your companion and they can't do that unless they spend a lot of time with you.

NEIGHBORS

What is your relationship like with the people next door—good so far? If complaints are forthcoming about excessive barking, your dog invading their yard, breaking down their fence, jumping on their petunias, or threatening their children or pets, a very serious situation could erupt surprisingly fast.

CHILDREN

If a dog is already established in the household, he can be taught to live in harmony with a baby. But dogs and small children should never be left together without some responsible supervision. Unsupervised children account for a great many of the in-home injuries caused to and by pets. You will probably never know what painful and frightening experiences that a rescued dog has been through before you acquired him. You may find out a little by the way he reacts to certain objects or noises or even to some people, but you do not want to take the risk of triggering a past fear when the dog is alone with children.

Left: Helping take care of a dog is a good learning experience for a child.

CHOOSING
A DOG

Having decided that there is room, time, and money for a dog in your life, your next consideration has to be not only "I want a mixed breed or a crossbreed," but also what kind of dog, what sex, and what type of coat. These are crucial questions, apart from knowing whether you want a puppy or an adult.

TYPE OF COAT

If you want a long-coated pet, you have to enjoy grooming and you must have access to a place where you can do this twice-weekly chore. You will not want to groom a long-haired dog in your studio apartment, so where can the job be done on a winter's evening? Only you can

decide, but long coats do need attention if you are going to feel proud of your dog.

Puppies are not usually born with the type and length of coat that they will have when adult, so your only clue to what your dog will grow into is his mother. If the pup was not deliberately bred, then you probably have only half of the story, but that's what the luck of the mixed breed is all about.

Right: Thorough grooming is a soothing therapy for both the dog and his owner.

WHERE TO GET YOUR DOG?

There is never a shortage of dogs and puppies available from humane societies, animal shelters, and dog pounds. Even with the many improvements in animal control and in keeping strays off the streets in many places, there continue to be unwanted pups and adult pets. You can pick out a canine companion from any of hundreds in most towns. Many shelters have spay/neuter agreements that must be a part of any adoptions. Most shelter puppies and dogs also have had veterinary care including shots and checkups.

◆ When you choose an animal shelter as the source for your new dog or puppy you do two things right. You give a much needed home to what will probably become an excellent pet. You also support an organization that will help other pets find homes.

◆ Although it is possible to obtain a mixed breed dog or puppy from other sources, there are so many potential pets available in animal shelters that other sources should be only a last resort. Shelter pets usually come to their new adoptive homes with good health records, even if they don't have long pedigrees.

◆ Another source in your search is likely to be an advertisement for mixed breed puppies in a local newspaper. Be selective. It has to be faced that some dogs are kept in poor conditions, and the bitch may not have been well fed in pregnancy or during the time she is feeding the

Left: A healthy, well-groomed dog of good temperament is an object of pride for all the family.

puppies. A sickly puppy full of worms will need medical treatment. Harden your heart and walk away from the puppy if you have any doubts at all. If the dogs' conditions are awful, report them immediately to your local humane society. You may feel sorry for the puppies but buying a sick one could be both time-consuming and expensive. Sickly puppies are not easy to put right and such a pup may be prone to disease all his life.

◆ You can also try the local veterinary clinics. Sometimes the staff there may know of a mixed breed litter that is expected or already born. You will want to get your new puppy examined by a veterinarian anyway, as soon as you bring him home.

◆ Animal shelters and humane societies may have mixed breed puppies available, either born on the premises from bitches handed over because they are pregnant, or they may have puppies of about eight weeks old, the remnants of litters that the breeder could not place.

It is always helpful, when possible, to see the dam and to get a report on her attitude and behavior. Ask whether the puppies have been actively socialized, that is, had the opportunity to hear lots of different sounds and to see and be seen by many different types of people, so that they are aware of the wider world outside the litter.

SOCIALIZATION

Puppies should be socialized from about three weeks of age, and this usually means they are kept in an enclosed area, in a house or a busy part of a shelter. Puppies that are reared in an isolated kennel will tend to be fearful and more dog orientated than people orientated.

You want your puppy or dog to become a member of your human family. Find out as much as you can about the parentage of the pup you are considering.

ADULT SHELTER DOGS

Choosing an adult dog from a shelter is in some ways easier, as you can at least see the coat and the shape and size of the dogs. But will you ever know what the dog's previous life has been, what he has learned to be afraid of, or how he has been treated?

The staff of the shelter may have done some work with the dog and tried him out in a variety of situations, and with a number of different challenges. Even then, it may not be until you have had the dog in your own home for several weeks or even months that he reveals his true character. Always be vigilant, indoors and out, with your new adult pet, and never leave him alone with a baby or with small children until you are quite sure of his

Above: Rather than buy a puppy, you can acquire an adult dog from an animal shelter who is in need of a good home.

behavior in any given circumstances. The dog cannot tell you, in so many words, the fears and torments that he may have had to endure. You have to find out the hard way from his reactions. A few animal shelters will allow you to visit your prospective pet often and even to take the dog out on successive weekends until you are both really sure that you want to belong to each other.

ACQUIRING A PUPPY

So where will you get a puppy? The best place to start looking is at the animal shelters in your area. It may be hard to imagine that a puppy or a whole litter would be found at a shelter, but, in fact, many people turn their puppies over to shelters when they cannot find homes for them. It is not uncommon for a pregnant dog to be left at a shelter and to give birth there. Because dogs mate throughout the year, rather than seasonally, shelters are likely to have a selection of puppies at any time.

Generally, puppies are ready for adoption at about six to eight weeks of age, but if properly hand-raised, a puppy will not suffer if separated from his mother at birth. When choosing your mixed breed puppy from a shelter, remember that he does not necessarily resemble the adult dog that he will become. Some dogs change color as they mature. All puppies have floppy ears when born, but the ears may become erect over time. It is possible that the shelter staff has never seen the puppy's parents, so that the pup's heritage can only be a guess.

USEFUL TIPS

◆ Whatever the source of your puppy, make sure he has been wormed once or twice before you take him home, which will usually be when he is about eight weeks old.

◆ The puppy should be able to eat solid food, and should walk, run, and be ready to respond to your offer to play.

◆ If you have the choice of the litter, it may well be wise not to take the boldest one; "the one that comes toward you" used to be the received wisdom. Do not take a pup that hangs back and appears shy and reluctant to leave his bed.

◆ Choose the middle-of-the-range puppy, which should mean a dog that is not too dominant, nor too retiring. Never, ever, take a puppy that is obviously sick or is deformed in some way, just because your heart goes out to him and you feel

SPAYING A BITCH

If you take a bitch puppy from an animal shelter you will probably have to promise to get her spayed at a future date. Spaying a mixed breed bitch will save you all the worry of the times when she would come into season, and the unwanted attention of male dogs. Spayed bitches are also saved from life-threatening diseases of the uterus, and have a reduced risk of developing mammary cancers.

that he needs you. An unhealthy puppy will very likely grow up to be an unhealthy dog. Never begin your dog ownership with an unhealthy puppy; it is not fair to yourself, your friends, or the puppy. It is a mistake to think that imperfect puppies are going to be small, sweet, and compliant. Very often pain can trigger aggression and bad temper, and in addition there may be

difficulty with other dogs, who can be motivated to turn upon a weak member of the pack. You could be getting a lot of heartbreak and expense in trying to treat a puppy that never was sound.

PAYING FOR YOUR PUPPY

Animal shelters charge reasonable fees for puppy adoption. Adoption fees help to fund the care the puppy has received, but rarely cover the costs of actually running the shelter. Many shelters also have either spayed or neutered an adult dog already or have a reduced rate available for you to have your puppy spayed or neutered when it is old enough.

Left: Be prepared to search for the right puppy for your family and make sure that he is healthy and strong.

ACQUIRING AN ADULT DOG

Would you rather have an adult dog? There is plenty of choice, with young, middle-age, and even older mixed breed dogs in the shelters. You will probably find that the shelter staff insist that both male and female dogs are neutered before (or soon after) they leave their care.

To make your visits to local animal shelters most effective, you should make a list of qualities that you are looking for in your dog. Do you want a big dog who will enjoy jogging with you in the morning? Do you want a smaller dog to serve as a companion on the couch? Are you interested in grooming a dog with long hair, or would you prefer a lower-maintenance pet? Take as much time as you need at the shelters. Look at each dog, and keep your list at hand. You should take notes as you pass by each cage—if a dog meets your specifications, then write down his location and revisit him later.

There is no need to come home with a new pet the first day of your search. To select the right dog for you and your family is an important and permanent decision. Once you have chosen a dog, be prepared to answer the shelter staff's questions about your home, and your lifestyle. Although you may feel that these questions are somewhat intrusive, please be tolerant—animal shelters have a responsibility to place the dogs that come into their care in good, permanent homes with understanding owners.

It would be wrong to give the impression that taking an adult dog will be the easy option. This is unlikely to be true of a dog that has been running free, or has been abandoned by previous owners, or indeed has been brought to the animal shelter because he is unmanageable in some way.

Left: Taking your dog home is the beginning of a long, happy partnership.

Probably the kennel staff will have done some work with such a dog and will be able to tell you something about the way in which the dog behaves with other animals, and people: men, women, and children.

Spend some time with the dog that you are considering taking as a pet. Although the shelter staff may not be able to accommodate you, try to take the dog around the shelter on your own and to evaluate him using the following steps.

ASSESSING A SHELTER DOG'S TEMPERAMENT

1 Try to have the dog you are attracted to in a separate room with no more than two adults present (not kennel staff). Children should not be included.

2 Sit quietly for ten minutes, not speaking to the dog, but watching his reaction to you. Do not make eye contact. See if he is curious enough to approach you.

3 Extend the back of your hand to the dog for him to sniff.

4 If the dog appears interested and friendly, look at him while you offer your hand again.

5 Offer a small piece of biscuit. Does the dog fear you, does he snatch the food, does he refuse? These reactions do not preclude taking the dog; they indicate the areas you will have to work on.

6 If the dog is friendly toward you, squat down and see if he will come to you. Offer a tug toy and see if the dog is confident enough to play.

7 At another testing
session, come in very
nonchalantly while
brandishing a walking
stick or an umbrella.
Does the dog panic?

8 Make a loud
noise by
banging lightly on
a metal object or
something similar.

9 Ask if you may observe the dog's
behavior when he is outside in a run
with some other dogs.

10 Ask the staff if they have had the
dog in the reception area or in the
recreation room with them.

11 Try putting a lead
on the dog and try
to talk him into going
out with you.

12 Take the dog
for a short
walk, put him back
into the kennel, and
then invite him to
come out again.

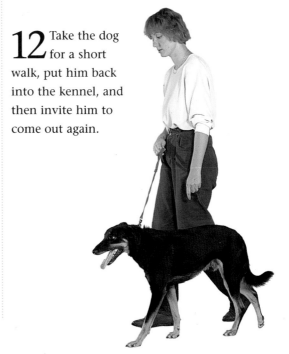

◆ All the while, without appearing to focus on the dog, you will be observing his behavior patterns—not expecting any kind of perfection but looking for any negative reactions that may have to be overcome. Only after you have won the dog's confidence will you feel you can introduce children of various ages. Expect to make these exploratory meetings over a period of days. When you find that the dog is looking out for you and really pleased to see you, you will realize that you have the basis of a good dog/human relationship.

◆ Dogs recognize tone of voice and facial expressions, so keep your voice light and happy even if the dog shows hostility. Dogs detect body postures of uncertainty, so your approach must always be warm, light, and inconsequential. If the dog is constantly unfriendly, make no response and walk away; never show anger that your offer of friendship has been rejected.

◆ Try again on another day and continue until the dog is used to seeing you and has convinced himself that you mean him no threat and no harm.

Above and right: Spend lots of time playing with your new puppy and getting to know each other. Make a fuss of him and reward him with cuddles when he obeys your commands.

PUPPY HEALTH CONCERNS

Puppies are born in a very unfinished state, without sight or hearing, and needing the stimulation of their dam's tongue in order to urinate or defecate. Puppies are able to cry, and to crawl on their abdomens, but are not capable of keeping themselves warm unless they are adjacent to a source of heat. At birth their lungs are immature and their hearts have a lot of adjustment to make. Within three to four weeks, however, those same puppies will have developed into active, all-seeing, all-hearing, all-barking little characters, being weaned onto solid food, anxious to explore their environment and everything within it. Another week will have them playing actively with the rest of the litter, and with toys, growling, barking, and responding to the sound of their breeder's voice. At this stage they can recognize their own need to pass urine and feces and will be motivated to move away from their sleeping area to do so. In fact, the puppies have reached the stage, well within two months, that we might expect a human baby to reach at two years old.

HEALTH PROBLEMS

Some of the puppies may be born with imperfections, possibly due to an infection that the bitch may have picked up while they were developing in the uterus. Often defects are not noticed until the puppies begin to be active. Examine them carefully for any imperfections before you make your choice.

◆ HERNIAS

Probably the most common congenital defects are hernias, either at the navel (an umbilical hernia) or in the groin (an inguinal hernia). A hernia is a protrusion of a part of the body's organs through a weakness in the surrounding tissue. There may be a need for a surgical repair later on if the hernia grows larger.

◆ CLEFT PALATE

A cleft palate is the result of a failure of the hard palate, on the roof of the mouth, to fuse properly. The breeder will no doubt have noticed early on that the puppy was unable to suck properly from the bitch, and may have been very difficult to rear and appear under-nourished in comparison with the rest of the litter. The breeder is the best person to cope with a puppy with a major defect such as this; do not be persuaded into taking such a puppy, even as a gift.

◆ CHEST PROBLEMS

When you pick a puppy up, you may hear a wheezing or rattling sound in his chest. This may be because his lungs may not have expanded properly at birth, or because fluid has got down into the chest. Ask for a veterinary examination before deciding to take on such a puppy.

◆ LAMENESS
Often puppies are a little unsteady on their feet at first, but let the puppy you are considering run about on the floor alone and watch carefully for persistent lameness on one leg, or a tendency to fall over frequently. Leave this puppy at the shelter.

◆ JUVENILE PYODERMA
This is a rash of tiny pus-filled spots often on the hairless parts of the abdomen or in the groin. This is thought to be caused by a failure of the bitch to clean the puppies sufficiently well, or possibly comes from the use of old newspaper as bedding for the puppies. The rash should clear up with more attention to hygiene and bathing with antiseptic lotion, but antibiotics may be needed also. Ask for veterinary advice before buying the puppy. You will usually find the whole litter has the rash. This may be a reason for taking your puppy away as early as seven weeks of age in order to improve his living conditions.

◆ BODY TREMORS
Many puppies shake and twitch while they are asleep; this is natural and is thought to be connected with the developing nervous system. However, a state of low blood sugar, brought on by stress and excitement, may cause whole body tremors that may lead to convulsions. This condition may occur during play when the puppy first changes homes and is made an object of everyone's attention. Convulsions are usually the sign of a more serious condition. Take the pup immediately to your veterinarian.

◆ THE URINARY SYSTEM
Sometimes the urinary system may be imperfectly developed in puppies, but this condition might go unnoticed while the pups are together in the litter. A constant

uncontrolled dribbling of urine may result from a defect in the urinary system so that urine produced in the kidneys by-passes the bladder and consequently it cannot be stored. This condition, which tends to occur in female puppies, can be corrected by surgery. Urine scalding on the abdomen of a puppy is painful and unpleasant. The cause should be investigated by a veterinarian.

◆ DIGESTIVE SYSTEM
When you go to see puppies around six weeks of age, see if you can arrange to be there when they are fed. Pups of this age are usually fed from a communal dish, so watch which ones are greedy and which seem reluctant to eat. Puppies always defecate soon after their meal, and this is an important clue to the health of the litter. The bowel movements should be formed, not loose, unless the pups have been wormed that day. Diarrhea is a common but undesirable condition in puppies. There may be many causes for this: possibly a change of diet, unwise feeding, a heavy worm infestation, the result of a worming dose, or a disease, such as the easily transmissible canine parvovirus. If the whole litter is seen to pass loose, blood-stained feces, go no further with your interest in getting one of these puppies and please disinfect your shoes and clothes before visiting any other breeders.

Canine parvovirus is a dreadful disease and is very difficult to eradicate once it is endemic in a shelter or kennel.

Do not take away a puppy that is producing loose stools, but, as this may only be a temporary state, arrange to visit again in three or four days.

INFECTIOUS DISEASES

Are eyes and nose running with mucus? Distemper is still a very real disease. Kennel cough may also be present where there is a constantly changing population of dogs. This airborne virus is easily transmissible and it can last a very long time and even be fatal in puppies.

The typical cough sounds as if the dog has got something stuck in his throat. Your new pet may get over a cough quickly, but if his cough lingers, he should be seen by a veterinarian.

FEEDING YOUR DOG

Do not be tempted to feed your dog or puppy on demand. A greedy dog will keep on eating, and you must control your dog's weight. Here are some general guidelines to help you.

FEEDING A PUPPY

◆ As a general rule, most eight-week-old puppies are fed four times a day, reducing to three times (but increasing the quantity given) at twelve weeks old.

◆ An average quantity of food at each meal for an eight-week-old pup would be 5 oz. (150 g) of premium dry puppy food.

◆ Keep the feeding times regular and always provide clean, fresh water. Puppies should *never* be fed cow's milk.

◆ For puppies, it is best to avoid feeding any table scraps. Such human foods can upset a puppy's balanced diet.

◆ Make sure that no other animal can take the pup's food and ensure that he does not feel threatened while he is eating.

◆ If, after 10 to 20 minutes, the puppy has not eaten all the food in his dish, remove it and throw it away. Do not give him anything else to eat until the next feeding time becomes due.

◆ Sometimes puppies have sore mouths when they are cutting their second teeth—at four to six months of age. Moistening dry food can make it much easier for the puppy to chew.

FEEDING AN ADULT DOG

◆ The easiest way to feed your adult dog is to use commercially prepared canned or dried foods from a leading manufacturer. There are feeding instructions on the packaging and most companies also employ specialist nutritionists whom you can consult if you have problems.

◆ Many owners feel that they must offer a dog as much variety of food as they have themselves, but this is a fallacy. If a dog likes a particular dried or canned food, he will eat it every day for most of his life.

◆ Some owners add a few household scraps to enliven a dried diet, but the dog does not really need them. If you do give your dog table scraps, be certain to include them in the overall determination of how many calories he is consuming.

◆ A medium-sized adult dog will eat one to one-and-a-half standard-sized 12 oz. (376 g) cans of meat and an equal volume of biscuits every day, divided into two meals. A benefit of using quality commercially prepared diets is that they contain a perfect balance of essential vitamins and minerals. You have no need to add more.

◆ Dogs are usually fed twice a day: morning and evening. The timing should be kept as regular as possible.

◆ If you are feeding a dried food, you will

notice that your dog drinks more than when on a softer diet. The dry food acts as a cleaner for the teeth and gums, but some dogs do prefer their meals to be moist, so soak the dry food in some water, stock or thin gravy before feeding.

◆ Food refusal in a healthy dog is always a matter for concern, but one day does not really matter except in a very young puppy. Pain, shown by rolling and moaning, or by going into the prayer position (down on his front legs but with the abdomen elevated and the hind legs in standing attitude) should not be allowed to continue. Telephone your veterinarian immediately.

◆ Some dogs are fussy eaters. For instance, some will not eat when there are unfamiliar people in the house, or when there is excessive noise. In some dogs, guarding comes first, and food can wait until the assumed danger is over. Some male dogs will stop eating temporarily when a bitch close-by is in season.

◆ You may notice that your dog is only willing to take food into one side of his mouth. Take him to the veterinarian at once so that the condition can be properly investigated.

◆ Sick dogs appreciate having their food softened. A sick pet may not readily eat. Feeding a sick pet requires patience, tenderness, and a call to the veterinarian for advice. Hand-feeding is often necessary when dogs are very ill. They will take food from the owner's hand when they will not eat it off a plate.

FEEDING AN ELDERLY DOG

◆ Old dogs need special care and often special meals. You may find that your dog prefers four small meals a day rather than two large ones, and that liquidized or very finely chopped food is more acceptable.

◆ Teeth can be painful or there may be growths in the mouth, so do not expect your geriatric friend to eat hard dog biscuits.

◆ Older dogs need less protein than growing animals in order to relieve stress on their aging kidneys. The brand of food you have been using may be available in a special formula for older dogs.

◆ Some older dogs suffer from arthritis of the spine and they find bending to the floor to eat very uncomfortable. It is possible to buy metal bowl stands that raise the food bowl 7–8 in. (17.5–20 cm) above floor level.

THE HEALTHY ADULT DOG

The health of adult dogs is easy to check. Look for clear eyes, reasonably sweet breath, clean teeth, and a good clean coat. Bright pink mucus membranes inside of ears and lips are not good signs, especially in a white dog, which may be suffering from an allergy that is expensive to diagnose and treat.

One feature that is important to check in male puppies over three months old and in adult dogs is whether there are two testicles that are descended into the scrotum. The testicles normally come down when the puppy is between six and twelve weeks old, and sometimes even older, but occasionally, one testicle is permanently retained in the abdominal cavity, and there is the possibility that this testicle can become cancerous. Many veterinarians will suggest that a retained testicle be removed surgically before it gives any trouble.

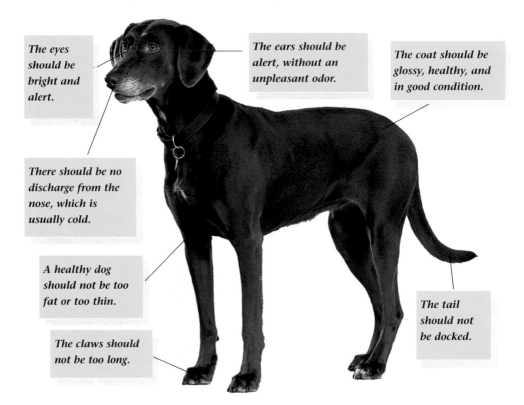

The eyes should be bright and alert.

The ears should be alert, without an unpleasant odor.

The coat should be glossy, healthy, and in good condition.

There should be no discharge from the nose, which is usually cold.

A healthy dog should not be too fat or too thin.

The tail should not be docked.

The claws should not be too long.

PUPPY MAINTENANCE

Get ready for your new puppy or your dog well ahead of the proposed homecoming. You can start by checking out your home and yard thoroughly to ensure that everything is safe and secure.

YOUR YARD

◆ Check your fencing, remembering that puppies can squeeze through very small holes and will also dig under wire or wooden fencing. Ideally the fence should be inserted 6 in. (15 cm) into the ground.
◆ Check access to any water features in the yard, such as ponds and swimming pools. Ideally, they should be fenced in or surrounded by walls.
◆ Make sure that any poisonous substances, such as slug bait, insecticides, herbicides, or other poisons are on very high shelves in your shed or garage. Check also that none of the poisons have been laid around your yard. Weed killer is especially dangerous. The packaging of some slug baits and pesticides may state that the preparation is safe to use where there are household pets, but you cannot be too careful, and puppies will eat anything to excess. Many of the slug preparations have a sweet taste that dogs seem unable to resist. Antifreeze liquid, and anything containing lead, such as old paint, can be poisonous.
◆ The seeds, flowers, and bark of the laburnum tree have been known to cause fatalities in pets. Flower bulbs, such as

daffodils and hyacinths, are dangerous and are just the kind of thing that a puppy will chew. At Christmastime beware of the berries of holly and mistletoe, and the leaves of the poinsettia plant.

◆ Take a look at access to any roads from your yard. Fence the front yard as well as the back, and check that the gate catches. They should shut easily and quickly behind callers so that the pup has no opportunity to slip out. Take particular care of the security of any gate between the front and the back of your house, especially if it is used by other people.

◆ This is the time to clear away piles of disused materials, such as old cans of paint, discarded wood with nails sticking out, old car batteries, and plastic containers that once contained corrosive material. You may be sure the puppy will get at anything you do not want him to. Be sure that there are no shards of broken glass or china near the surface of the earth. Make every effort to check your yard for anything that could do harm to your new pet. Look for sharp edges, protruding wires, live electrical wires that could be chewed on, antifreeze spills, and other things that could hurt or kill a curious dog or puppy.

◆ Keep the puppy indoors when you are using any sprays on plants or spreading any fertilizers. Puppies and adult dogs do tend to eat horse manure spread on the garden, but it seems to do them no harm.

INDOOR HAZARDS

Indoors, beware of electrical connections. Make sure that there are no dangling cords or plug points at floor level that the puppy can reach.

◆ Kitchen cupboards must be fitted with secure fastenings or you may come home to find that the puppy

Left: Woven baskets are difficult to clean and get destroyed very easily. A plastic bed is a better choice for durability.

book that get chewed. The habit of not leaving possessions around has to be learned by adults and children alike, because it is unfair to be angry with the puppy for tearing up something that could just as easily have been put out of his reach.

has created a mixture of raw potatoes, sugar, flour, and beans—not a good idea!

◆ The cupboard under the sink, where cleaning fluids and soaps are kept, is particularly dangerous. Dogs are attracted by soap, so make sure that none is accessible in the bathroom, laundry room, or kitchen. A bar of soap taken into the mouth and foaming up when mixed with saliva can choke a dog to death.

◆ Make sure that the puppy cannot get at the washing machine outlet. Many hoses are chewed through by pups.

◆ When leaving a puppy alone in the kitchen or utility room, it is best to turn off the source of electricity from all apparatus, and never leave electrical equipment plugged into the sockets.

◆ Puppies and dogs are most likely to chew the articles that their owner has handled recently. This is why it is always the new shoes or the most recently read

TOYS

◆ A puppy needs lots of suitable toys, just as a child does. Buy toys that are sturdy and tough, designed and created for dogs. Be especially wary of toys that include squeakers; these may overexcite

CHOKING

If you play with your dog with a ball, make sure it is of a size that is too big to obstruct the back of his throat—choking on a ball is not uncommon and requires immediate first aid. Get behind the dog and with one hand on each side of the head, push forward sharply so that the ball is ejected. Trying to reach inside the mouth does little to help, as there is too much saliva, and it is dangerous for both you and your dog.

a puppy or dog that has terrier ancestry, as the squeak can invoke a killing instinct. Squeakers are easily removed from toys and may be swallowed, causing serious damage to the dog.

◆ A piece of cotton cloth that is large enough not to be swallowed gives great pleasure to a puppy, as does a length of tough rope for tugging games.

GATES, PENS, AND CRATES

◆ A baby gate can be invaluable in confining a puppy in a room without shutting him away from human company. It can also be used at the bottom of the stairs to stop the puppy from rampaging all over the bedrooms. If he does scramble upstairs, help him to come down safely until he is big enough to cope on his own.

Baby gates and folding wire crates help to confine the pup to certain areas of the house safely. Puppies need to be able to see other people and hear lots of sounds while being absolutely secure from harm. A wire crate is an ideal investment, used as a

Above: A pen can be a comfortable and safe den for a young puppy.

bed and as a den, with the door open so that the puppy can go in and out as he wishes, or with the door closed as a temporary safety zone when there is activity in the house that might lead to a dangerous situation for him. Never confine the puppy to the crate for long periods. Encourage your family to always maintain a positive attitude about the crate.

BEDS AND BEDDING

Your pet will always do better if taught to sleep in his crate. This allows the dog or puppy to sleep in the place that has become his "den" or own special place within your home. Make the crate more comfortable by placing a washable crate pad of the right size in the crate. These pads, available at most sellers of pet products, are much better than old blankets, towels, or discarded clothing. Never put food or water in the crate. This will only make a mess. The crate is for relaxation and sleeping. Eating and drinking need another location. Always keep a pet's crate as clean as possible. Keep it out of direct sunlight and away from drafts.

Above: Your dog should have a leather or cotton collar with a name tag and a leather or cotton lead. Braided nylon could be substituted for leather, but chain collars should be used only for training purposes.

COLLAR AND LEAD

◆ You also need a leather collar of an appropriate size for an adult dog, or a softer collar for a puppy. With these collars go leather leads with secure hooks.

◆ An extending lead, contained in a box handle, that you can let out or pull in at will can be useful if you want to give a confirmed roamer a little more range, but it should never be used in urban areas as they can easily prove an obstruction and cause an accident.

IDENTITY TAGS

Possibly your most important buy of all is a name tag engraved with your name and telephone number. Without this important information, your puppy or dog becomes just another homeless stray. With this information, you have a much better chance of getting your pet back. Many of the pets advertised as "Lost" in the newspaper would be more easily found.

A name tag with your current address can save your dog's life, so check on it often, to ensure that the engraving is still legible. Most pet stores, shelters, or veterinarians will be able to direct you to a source of name tags.

MICROCHIPPING

Thousands of pets are lost every year—a tragedy that can happen to the most careful owner.

Many of these animals are never reunited with their owners. The best way to avoid losing your pet is to have him implanted with a specially developed microchip "tag." This provides a permanent link between you and your pet.

The chip's code is held on a computer network that keeps a record of an owner's name and address. Many veterinary clinics and others have scanners that can read the microchip's code.

Microchipping is no more complicated than a normal injection. A tiny microchip—the size of a grain of rice—is inserted under your pet's skin. The cost can vary but it is not expensive. Contact your veterinarian if you decide to have your dog microchipped.

GROOMING EQUIPMENT

A pet store will also help you to choose the right type of brush and comb for your dog's coat. Even if your puppy does not have much coat to groom, start doing it regularly from the time he comes to you so that grooming time will become an enjoyable habit for you both.

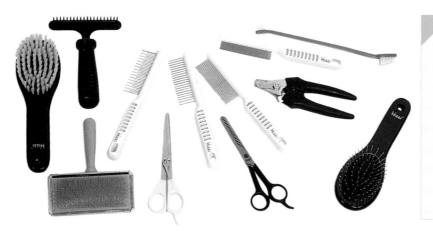

Left: You will need grooming tools to remove dead hair from your dog's coat. Ask your veterinarian or a professional groomer which are most suitable for your dog. Use a toothbrush to clean his teeth and ask how to cut his nails.

CREATING CONFIDENCE

One of your primary tasks is to give your puppy or your adult dog confidence in you and other people. Puppies are most impressionable between eight and twelve weeks old, and the experiences encountered at this time must all be happy ones.

◆ You will obviously need to prevent a puppy from doing damage to your furnishings but do it in a positive way; distract the pup with a food treat and direct his attention to some occupation that is permissible. You may well have to do the same thing for an adult dog that has spent some time in an animal shelter.

◆ Always speak to your dog in a happy voice—never shout—and praise your dog or puppy when he comes to you when you call him.

◆ You, first of all, and members of your family and callers to your home must all be good news for your dog.

◆ Never allow anyone to tease the dog or pretend to threaten him. Such behavior could have dangerous consequences, particularly if you have a dog who has had a bad time in his past.

THE LANGUAGE

You must have just one more family conference before you collect the puppy that is to be yours. Perhaps you need not decide on the puppy's name until he is in your home so that you can choose something really appropriate, but do decide on the other words you are going to use to train the puppy so that everyone in the household, or those who are going to meet the puppy, will be talking the same language. Puppies respond to sounds, so you must all use the same ones.

Which words will you use for "Come here," "Go away," "Lie down," "Sit," and for the all-important housebreaking sequence? It is sensible not to use nursery terminology

here, as passersby may be amused. Your task in retraining an adult dog may be difficult, due to the time he has spent in shelters. Consistency is the secret; take him to the same spot every time and wait around, offering him encouragement, until he performs, then be lavish with your praise.

If your dog should defecate in the street or in a public open space, never reproach him. Be ready with a small plastic bag over your hand to scoop up the mess and pop the bag and contents into a plastic carrier. Tie the handles together, ready to put into the first appropriate garbage can. When you are house-training your puppy at home, you should follow the same regime. Any urine

or defecation mistakes your dog may make inside *must* be thoroughly cleaned up with a cleaner that blocks out the residual odor. Dogs have a sense of smell vastly more acute than that of humans. They can scent any places where they have relieved themselves if these places haven't been deodorized. Because dogs are creatures of habit, when they get a smell of where they went once, they are most likely to go there again. Use a good, proven odor neutralizer to eliminate all scent traces.

BRINGING YOUR PUPPY HOME

It is best to arrange to bring home your puppy or your adult dog in the morning, and then you will have the whole day to get acquainted. Many people do this on a Saturday so that they have the whole weekend. Some take a week's vacation to get to know their puppy.

◆ You should have inquired ahead of time as to what food the puppy has been weaned on, so that you can get a supply of the food to which it is accustomed. It is wise to keep the puppy on this food. Never change your puppy's food unless you are having some food-related problem and on the advice of a veterinarian. If your pet is doing well on its regular diet, don't upset its system and eating habits by changing to something else. If a change in food ever becomes necessary, as from puppy food to adult food, make the change gradually. Mix more and more of the new food with less and less of the old food over a seven to ten day period.

◆ The biggest change for the puppy will be in getting used to being a single individual instead of one of a number of puppies. Whatever the pleasures you can offer, the loss of the companionship and

VACCINATION

All puppies must be vaccinated against the following dangerous infectious diseases:
- Distemper
- Canine parvovirus
- Hepatitis
- Leptospirosis
- Rabies
- Borelliosis
- Parainfluenza

These vaccines are usually given in a two- or three-stage course. You may find that your eight-week-old puppy has had only the first injection and your own veterinarian will have to complete the course. Adult dogs should also have annual boosters for the same diseases as immunity does wane in time. It may be that you will be told that your puppy has been vaccinated and you will be required to pay for this protection. Make sure that you receive a proper printed vaccination certificate that has been signed by a veterinarian.

It is best not to rely on homeopathic vaccination routines; this is one area of homeopathy that is not always effective and this type of vaccination is generally not accepted by boarding kennels. They won't take in dogs which haven't had conventional vaccinations.

support of others is deeply felt. However, so is the compounded excitement of being in a new environment and with new people. Always keep the food and the feeding times to what the puppy has been used to. The same advice will also apply to an adult dog.

THE JOURNEY HOME

It is usual to bring home a puppy or adult dog by car and this is much easier if there are two people involved. If you are alone, put the puppy in a plastic travel kennel.

For the journey home, take with you a towel to cover your lap, a roll of paper towels to clean up accidents, and a small dish and a bottle of water if the trip is at all long. Try to make the trip home as untraumatic as possible. You don't want to instill a fear of traveling in your pet. Do not let an adult dog or pup out of your control on the way home—you do not belong to him yet and he is very likely to run off.

ARRIVING HOME

Resist the temptation to take your puppy to show friends and relatives, or to ask them to come around when you get home. Take things slowly; do not overwhelm the puppy, or the adult dog for that matter, with new experiences all on the same day.

Give your new pet time to adjust to you, your family, and your house, and keep excitement to a minimum. Let the dog explore on his own while you watch discreetly. Call him back to you often. If you have a small puppy, go down to his level and welcome him with open arms—your delight in each other will be mutual.

FIRST NIGHTS
Probably the first crisis in a young puppy's life will come at the end of the first day with you. He may have fallen into several deep sleeps during the day, but by nightfall he should

Left: When you arrive home, spend some time getting to know your new puppy.

HEALTH CHECKS

You would be wise to take your new puppy to a veterinarian for a checkup. Many people arrange to go to the veterinarian on their way home with the puppy. The advantage is that you can be assured that the puppy is sound and healthy, and if a major fault is found, you can take it back to the shelter right away without the risk of taking infectious disease into your home.

Ask the veterinarian about anti-flea and tick treatments for both the puppy and your home. Controlling fleas means all-out war against them. You must remember that fleas can get on and off your pet *anywhere* that the dog may go; the house, the doghouse, the yard, the car, the crate, the cottage at the lake. If you are to eradicate fleas, *each* place the dog inhabits must be treated, including the dog itself!

Fleas, ticks, and other canine-borne external parasites can also affect humans. Some humans, like some dogs, can have extreme allergic reactions to the bite of a single flea. Scabies mites cause mange in dogs and can affect humans. Ticks can spread several diseases.

be worn out by his many new experiences. You may settle the puppy in his cage or crate with a well-covered hot water bottle for a very young puppy to cuddle up to.

One of the most traumatic experiences for puppies, and puppy owners, can be the first few nights in the pup's new home. The puppy is understandably afraid in a new setting. It is important that the puppy's owners set some rules now that will shape the future for this new pet.

Always let the puppy go to sleep in its own crate. Be very strict with your family and yourself about anyone hearing the lonely youngster and taking it out of its designated sleeping place. Your puppy

will be afraid and may cry the first few nights but it must learn that crying won't get it any attention. Many adult shelter

dogs never learned this lesson and sad, crying puppies became sad, crying adults.

Canines won't want to mess up their sleeping area with urine and feces. Be certain that the puppy is taken out right before bedtime and again as early as possible the next morning. Many puppies will need to relieve themselves during the middle of the night and you may have to get up and let your puppy out. This need will probably subside by the age of four months.

Health and Condition

The eyes are a very good indicator of a dog's condition. Runny eyes or a nose exuding mucus demand instant advice. Telephone the veterinarian for an appointment.

◆ Run your hands over your dog frequently, identifying lumps and bumps. Is it a tick embedded in the flesh? Is it a wart or another skin condition? Do not let any blemish go unnoticed for long.

◆ An invasion of parasites may be the cause; or there may be an ear or tooth disease. Get a diagnosis quickly before the condition becomes chronic.

Parasites

Most cities and towns allow dog feces to be put into garbage cans. Dispose of all fecal material properly. Dogs, like other mammals including humans, are prey to internal parasites. Roundworms attack the health and vitality of puppies. Maintain a clean environment to keep roundworms and other parasites away from your pet. Always dispose of feces quickly and in an appropriate manner. When you have your pup checked out by a veterinarian make certain that it is wormed for roundworms, hookworms, and tapeworms. The mosquito-introduced heartworm will need to be dealt with after the pup is older. Remember that some parasites, like roundworms, can be transmitted to children and adults.

It is important to worm dogs and puppies regularly and to dispose of the excreta effectively. It is best to get the worming preparation from a veterinary clinic so that you get a dosage that is effective but not so strong as to upset the dog. Whereas it is possible to buy wormer remedies, if you let this treatment be handled by your veterinarian you will be certain of its effectiveness and your pet's health. The best approach is to let your veterinarian check for parasites and then treat any infestations that are found.

In many parts of the United States, heartworms are introduced into dogs by infected mosquitoes. Heartworms literally clog a dog's heart and cause a painful, early death. Your veterinarian will help you get your pet on a heartworm preventative.

FEEDING

It is usual to feed eight-week-old puppies four times daily, with clean water always available for drinking. Puppies do not need milk; in fact, it can bring on diarrhea. The choice of foods lies mainly with quality puppy foods which are labeled "complete," which means you do not need to give anything else; or dried complete foods, which are usually lightly moistened with warm water for puppies.

◆ You will find that many brands of dog food provide a range of "age-designed" foods, that is, for growing puppies, adult dogs, and elderly dogs.

◆ It is easier for the owner and better for the puppy to feed a commercially formulated

WORMING

A puppy should have been wormed at least once, preferably twice, before he leaves his first home. Ask the breeder or shelter staff when he was wormed and which preparation was used, so that you can tell your vet when you take the puppy for his first health check and vaccination.

It is possible that even if a worming preparation was given, the puppy may have brought it up again. It will usually be necessary to worm the puppy again, but wait until the vet can weigh him and prescribe the appropriate dose. Your pet should be checked for worms during each veterinary visit.

food that is balanced with all the necessary vitamins and minerals, and that carries instructions about the quantity to feed on the label. If in doubt, your veterinarian will advise.

◆ Keep a close eye on your new puppy or adult dog during the first few days and weeks. Diarrhea is probably the most alarming sign that all is not well with a pup. You may be giving too much food, or too many unsuitable treats.

◆ Your new pet will depend solely on you to provide its every need. Good dog food, a safe environment, affection, training, and daily attention are all obvious needs. You will also be the first line of medical defense for your dog or puppy's health. Only by paying attention to indicators like diarrhea, vomiting, loss of appetite, and signs of pain and discomfort can you do this part of your job as dog owner correctly. Pay close attention to your pet's health on a daily basis. If you see that your dog has gone into the "prayer position," with its front legs stretched out before it and the abdomen and back legs held high, call

Above: Dog diets labeled "complete" come in various textures, and with a balanced content for growing puppies and adults. A good brand will contain all the protein, fat, carbohydrates, vitamins, and minerals that your dog needs at every stage of his life.

your veterinarian immediately. Your dog may have swallowed something that is causing an obstruction in its stomach.

◆ Your role will be to observe the color and firmness of your pet's stools. You will have to recognize dull coats, nasal discharge, and other possible danger signals. You will have to develop a good relationship with your veterinarian, the next line of medical defense.

◆ If the diarrhea is persistent or if the puppy becomes ill, you should take him to the vet immediately. If vomiting accompanies the diarrhea, you should seek veterinary advice.

THE VETERINARIAN AND YOUR PET

Next to you, your dog will have to depend on your veterinarian to help it stay healthy, to treat illnesses that may arise, and to handle any accidents or emergencies that may occur. The veterinarian is a true professional, as skilled as any other physician in preventing and treating disease, and repairing injuries. The fact that a veterinarian works with animals should not in any way lessen the respect that should be afforded this valued healing arts practitioner. You can help your veterinarian care for the medical needs of your pet:

◆ Make certain that your dog or puppy has all the vaccinations it should have, when it should have them,

◆ Keep the place where the dog lives as safe as possible,

◆ Avoid situations and conditions that could injure or even kill your pet,

◆ Make certain that your pet has regular checkups with the veterinarian,

◆ Follow the veterinarian's instructions about medicines and other remedies precisely!

◆ Do not delay taking your pet to the veterinarian should an illness seem likely or in the event of an accident.

Finding the right veterinarian may be as simple as visiting the clinic closest to your home. You can also contact your local veterinary association for the names of qualified practitioners near your home. Many people ask their dog-owning friends, especially in places where there are several animal hospitals, which of these they may recommend. Local kennel and dog training clubs may have a list of veterinarians they recommend.

Veterinarians are like all other kinds of professionals. Some veterinarians will be better suited to your needs than others. The way to make a realistic assessment of whether a certain practitioner will be better for you than another is to know what you want and need. You may also decide that you want to choose a veterinarian solely on the basis of his or her personality. Know what you want and your decision will be much simpler.

When you visit a veterinary clinic, look for things that may be of added importance to you. Does the staff seem friendly and professional? Is the waiting room area convenient and clean? Is it overcrowded? Is there more than one veterinarian in attendance? Does this clinic provide coverage during off-hours? Does the entire facility make you feel uncomfortable or ill at ease, or does it radiate concern and caring about you and your pet?

BEHAVIOR AND TRAINING

Whether you have acquired a puppy or an adult dog, your pet has to learn some important lessons if he is to settle into his new home and to become a much-loved member of your family. However, like people, all dogs are individuals and some learn more quickly than others. Your dog will have to be house-trained and learn to respond to your voice and your commands.

HOUSEBREAKING A PUPPY

Begin housebreaking with the knowledge that no matter how much your puppy may want to please you by not messing up in the house, on average a puppy will have limited bladder control until it is about six months old. You don't need to wait that long to start, but you do need to realize that some mistakes will happen purely because of the physical immaturity of your new puppy.

You actually can begin this important training the very day you bring your puppy home from the shelter or other source. Have a preselected relief area set aside for the puppy's ongoing use. When

you arrive home, even before you go inside, go to the relief spot and wait until the youngster urinates or defecates there. When it does (and it eventually will!) give the pup lots of love and praise for doing the right thing in the right place. This positive reinforcement is crucial to the success of your housebreaking efforts. Without it, the puppy may not quickly catch on that doing what it needs to do really pleases you when it does it at the relief spot.

Crate training will greatly aid in housebreaking because your puppy will instinctively not want to mess up in the place where it sleeps. By going out early in the morning, late at night, and after the puppy eats or drinks, you can pretty effectively stop most little accidents before they happen. Going out after each meal or drink is important because the youngster doesn't yet have much capacity to hold substances inside. The added pressure on the bladder or colon just naturally causes a need to go out. You must be watchful, alert, and ready to get the young dog to the relief area. Even if

you don't quite make it, go on to the special spot and wait until the dog does go and then heap on lots of praise and petting.

Note: *Never* punish your dog or even speak harshly to him at the relief area. This is one place where you want nothing but positive experiences, so don't confuse the puppy at the relief spot.

At other times, when your puppy is inside with you, there are several signs that he may need to go out. These include the following:
◆ A general look of uneasiness
◆ Sniffing or nosing around for smells of where he might have gone before and could go again

Above: Young puppies, such as this Labrador-cross, are very inquisitive and love to explore their surroundings.

◆ Hanging around the door you use to go to the relief area or doing things to try to get your attention

If you see these signs, quickly take the pup out and give him enthusiastic praise. You have just seen your housebreaking efforts work.
◆ The alternative, if you really cannot cope with the outdoor excursions, is to make a thick pad of newspaper in the kitchen or another easily cleaned room and to put the puppy there when he shows his

PUNISHMENT

Punishing a puppy for making a mess indoors is not an effective training method. Punishing a puppy, especially with any of the very traditional and very wrong habits of rubbing his nose in the mess or swatting him with a rolled-up newspaper, will absolutely do nothing to help your puppy learn. In fact, such behavior could slow the learning process by frightening the youngster for following his own biological urges.

A puppy under six months old is going to have some bladder control immaturity and accidents will happen. Clean them up promptly and deodorize the places and reward the pup for doing right, not punish him for doing what he can't help.

intentions. Eventually, when he is a little older, you can move some sheets of used newspaper out into the yard and show the puppy where you wish him to go.

◆ Feces may be passed directly after eating, but different dogs have different biological schedules. Some dogs may need to go out one hour or two hours after a meal. You should chart your dog's eliminations and then base a schedule on the results.

◆ You can help to keep your house clean by not letting the puppy run through all the rooms; try to keep him in the utility part of the house until housebreaking is perfected.

◆ Try to develop a relief schedule that works for both you and your dog. You will be surprised at how quickly your puppy associates going outside with urination.

◆ When the house is soiled it will usually be close to the exit door, so always take the puppy out by the same door, and thereby help him to form a habit.

◆ At first you will have to carry the puppy but, as soon as it is practical, make him walk alongside you and wait while you open the door.

HOUSEBREAKING AN ADULT DOG

Depending on the individual adult dog, housebreaking may be relatively simple or it may be more difficult. Patience, as with puppies, will be the key here. Always try to get your pet outside, even if he is in the middle of a squat or leg hike. Go to the special spot that he uses and wait until he can go there and then give him lots of praise when he performs. You may see similar signs to when a puppy wants to go out (see page 65). Use these to help you aid your adult dog.

◆ Male dogs need to mark their territory, and this applies just as much to the neutered dog as the non-neutered one.

You may find that when your adult dog does go outside, he prefers to water a favorite shrub. It is best to leave this shrub in position and not to remove it even after it dies, because the marking point will be used again and again—every time the dog wants to emphasize his ownership.

◆ Be very careful not to punish the adult dog for misbehaving during house-breaking; it is important to you that you bond with the dog and that you both come to trust each other. Although you may feel that the dog should have known better, it can take a long time for an adult dog taken out of a shelter situation to realize that life is going to be different from now on.

Note: Never be tempted to rub a dog's nose in his waste. All this achieves is a dog with a smelly face and probably a simmering dislike of being handled by or even approached by his new owner. If your adult dog finds it easy to bark, you may want to encourage him to ask to go out; some dogs find it easy, whereas others never get the message and you have to think for them.

STAYING CLEAN OVERNIGHT

Your puppy will have two conflicting

Below: Keep your dog on a lead and under your control, especially when meeting other dogs.

instincts at work at night. He will not want to mess up his crate, and he won't be able to have enough bladder control to wait until morning. You may have to wake up in the middle of the night for awhile to see that the pup gets a relief break. Combine this with late night and early morning trips outside and most of the problem will resolve itself.

When accidents happen in the crate always thoroughly clean and deodorize it. This will help your pup not to become confused about where to relieve himself. Never put food or water in the crate because you won't be awake to know when the pup eats or drinks.

COMMUNICATING WITH YOUR DOG

Your dog needs a name that will be his name alone. Try not to have a dog name

CLEANING UP

There are many floor and carpet cleaners that you can use to clean up your dog's mess. The important thing is never to use anything containing ammonia, because that will compound the smell of urine so that the same spot will be used again. Disinfectant is useless on a soiled surface, so always wash well with some water and detergent first. Clean up thoroughly as any residual smell may trigger off repeat incidents. Odor eliminator sprays are available from your veterinarian.

that sounds like someone else's in the household, like Terry and Jerry. The dog's name is to get his attention, an event that may save the pet's life at some point in the future. Try to come up with a one- or two-syllable name that can be clearly understood. Encourage all members of your household to call the puppy by the same name. Nothing will confuse a young dog more than to be called by

one name and then another. When training your pet, the call name should always precede any command, as in "Buck, Sit," or "Buck, Heel."

OTHER VOCABULARY

After the puppy's name, "No" should be the most important word in his vocabulary. Say "No" to things that are definitely not permissible from the very first day that the puppy is in your home. If you saw the puppies with their dam, you may have observed that when they are tormenting the bitch, taking her food, or pushing her off the blanket, she will give a low growl and then if a pup persists, she will make one quick, loud snap close to him but without actually biting him. The snap is always made while the offense is being committed, and we know for sure that delayed admonition is always quite useless.

The word "No" when spoken in a firm and authoritative manner should be enough punishment for any pet. The fact that you, the Boss, are displeased with the puppy or dog should be all the discipline that a canine needs.

There is never an occasion when striking, slapping, or hitting the dog is called for. If you are using a chain collar during training times, a sharp pull on the lead should be all you need to get the dog to pay attention to you.

There are other attention-getting methods. For example, you could clap your hands together loudly, whistle, or toss a tin can filled with pebbles to break an errant puppy or dog's attention to doing some misdeed.

Corporal punishment can only cause the dog to distrust you. This is counter-training and works against the canine-human bond that you want to establish between you and your pet. You will be the center of your pet's universe. It is essential that you be fair, consistent, and concerned about the dog's well-being if you are to have the pet that you want.

TRAINING YOUR DOG

Train your dog or puppy to come to your call. Always use a happy voice and make coming to you worthwhile from the dog's point of view. You could try offering him a treat, a cuddle, or a little game.

◆ Dogs do what pays them best; if you are more fun than chewing the hose, your dog will come to you—it's as simple as that. Some experts recommend providing a food reward to produce the desired result, whereas others urge rewarding dogs with praise only. You should be consistent in whatever method you select.

◆ Don't shout at your dog. The dog who is constantly shouted at tends to take no notice at all, possibly thinking it is the normal human voice.

◆ In the beginning, the dog has to be eager to come to you. Later on, habit will take over and a pat and a smile will be reward enough.

◆ Call the puppy, always saying his name.

◆ Learn to read each other's facial expressions and body language. The dog will certainly learn about you, to such an extent that he will appear to read your mind before you have even made it up. Our dogs watch us constantly; they read gestures we did not even know we were making. Your facial expressions are important—making eye contact and smiling, even if you do not speak, makes your dog aware that all is right in both your worlds.

Below: Whenever your dog responds correctly in training, reward him with a treat, if desired, or a pat, or a cuddle.

SHORT DAILY SESSIONS

Experienced dog trainers believe in short training sessions. You should try to spend five minutes on dog education, say, three times a day, repeating what the dog was learning before, until connecting an action with the sounds that you make becomes an automatic reaction in your dog. Remember that your language is just "sound" to the dog. Before feeding the dog is usually a useful time to go through an "obedience" routine because then the dog's attention will be concentrated upon you. You should only elaborate on the basic training and introduce more advanced training when you feel that your dog is ready for it.

◆ In order to successfully teach your dog to come, there is one command that you must learn first—*never call your dog to you to do something bad to the dog.* One way to teach your dog not to come to you is to punish the dog after he has obeyed you. The next time you call him, the dog may hesitate or even ignore you. Make coming to you a happy occasion with lots of praise and affection. The dog wants to be with you, the added praise and petting merely reinforces his obedience to this all important command.

◆ Practice calling the dog back for a pat and a praise session and then letting him go again. If this does not work, he must be put on a very long rope, which trails behind him. When he will not come to your call, tread on the end of the rope and haul him in, rewarding him when he arrives.

Right: Your dog will want to please you, but some independent dogs may not always obey you!

"SIT"

The first, and easiest command, is the "sit." It makes a good starting point for all other obedience training. Some trainers teach dogs to sit by the "lure and reward" method, whereby a small food reward encourages the dog to obey the command. Others suggest using gentle pressure on a leash attached to the dog's chain collar to lift the dog's head upward while equally gentle pressure on the hindquarters causes the dog to sit. The verbal command "Sit" is given at exactly the same time that the two other parts of the command are given. Soon your dog will sit automatically when only the verbal command is given.

"DOWN"

◆ Sitting and offering a paw to "shake hands" is always endearing behavior. Alternatively, you may incorporate the "down" command by asking the dog to "sit," lie down, and then stand up again, just before you put the food bowl down.

Above: After your dog has mastered the "sit," this command can be used to get his attention or to go on to other commands.

Above: You should always discourage your dog from jumping up boisterously to greet you.

1

To teach "Down," if using food rewards, hold a tidbit in your closed hand.

2

Lower your hand to floor level and your dog will follow it until he is lying down.

◆ Never encourage a dog or puppy to jump up—either at yourself or at visitors and especially not at children. It is better to get down to the dog's level so that he can greet you more easily but this is not always convenient. Dogs have an inherited instinct to greet people by licks

GREETING ROUTINE

If you want to enjoy your dog to the fullest, you must invent a greeting routine that suits your particular situation, remembering that the dog has been looking forward to this homecoming from the minute after you left. Having something, such as a toy, to carry in the mouth diffuses an emotional moment.

on the mouth. This is really a throwback to the wild state, when the puppies would lick the bitch's mouth to get her to disgorge partially digested food for them. Indeed, this is still the habit with some young litters and is an action that is combined with the emotion of greeting and pleasure.

◆ Dogs will always delight in your arrival home, and, especially in the excitement of the moment, they can behave more exuberantly than we would like. Provide your dog with some acceptable way to welcome you. Throw a ball and let him bring it back to you—or give him a toy to carry away with great pride and a wagging tail. You could have a routine by which you come in and go straight to the biscuit jar and dispense a treat while the dog is put into the "sit" position. It does seem a pity to curb your dog's joy and exuberance by reacting with shouting.

"COME"

To teach your dog to come to you on command, he must first learn to "stay." Train him gradually over a period of time and always reward him when he does well.

1

1

Stand close to your dog, then back away slowly, repeating "Stay." Gradually increase the distance.

2

2

An open-arm welcome encourages your pet to come back to you.

3

3

A pat or a hug makes coming back to you worthwhile.

COLLARS AND LEADS

Put a soft collar on your puppy as soon as you acquire him, and do not forget that he should wear a dog tag engraved with your home telephone number and address, whenever he is away from home, even in the car. It is as well to let the puppy wear this tag on his collar during his first learning experiences, and then the dangling attachment will always be familiar to him. You can also consider a microchip (see page 53).

If you have obtained an adult dog from an animal shelter, he may already be equipped with a tag identifying the shelter he came from. It is best to remove this tag and substitute one with your own address right away. Then, if your dog should stray, there is every opportunity for the finder to get in touch directly with you. If a lost dog is taken in by an animal control officer and put into the care of kennels, there may be some delay in getting him back and you will have to pay a fee for his recovery and the care that he receives.

Train your puppy to wear the soft collar for short periods while he is being supervised. Your dog should wear a properly fitted buckle collar with identification tags at all times. A collar that is too loose can get caught on cupboard door handles. Training collars should be worn only when the dog is working.

LEAD-TRAINING
◆ Lead-training should begin in your yard or a park. Begin by putting a light lead on the puppy's collar and walking in the yard slowly, keeping the lead short and the puppy by your side, talking and encouraging him all the time. Never use an extending lead or a collar/lead combination for this lesson—a separate collar and a light lead will work best.
◆ When the puppy is walking reasonably by your side, progress to training on a pavement, but make the training session your only task at this time. Never try to lead-train when you are on an errand of any kind. Take a few minutes every day to concentrate on your dog, until he is walking at your side,

pulling neither forward nor backward.
◆ The concept of "walking to heel" is good for a companion dog to learn; keep the dog by your side with no tension on the lead at all. Pulling on the lead gets more difficult to eradicate as the weeks go by, but nothing looks more foolish than an owner being tugged along the road.
◆ Keep the lead short and if the dog pulls forward, turn around and go the other way until the dog is at your side again. You want your dog to neither pull ahead of you nor lag behind you. Pop the leash on the side of your leg to keep the dog's attention. Resist any impulse

Left: A well-trained dog walks quietly at his owner's side, with the owner holding the lead securely across her body in her right hand.

to tug on the dog's neck because this may cause injury to the internal structures of the neck. Persistence, practice, and reward will convey your message to the dog, and when you have achieved perfect lead walking you will have taught your dog and, incidentally, yourself something that will serve you both well all of your life together.

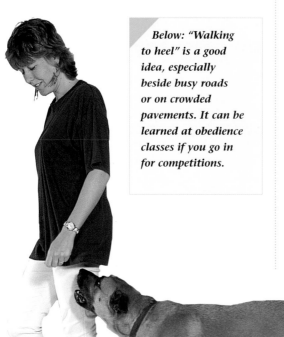

Below: "Walking to heel" is a good idea, especially beside busy roads or on crowded pavements. It can be learned at obedience classes if you go in for competitions.

CONTROLLING YOUR DOG

Always keep your dog on a short lead in a busy street. Do not let him approach other dogs or people unasked; nor should you allow children to shriek and shout when playing with a puppy. He will become overexcited and may even hurt someone or do some harm to himself in the process.

An adult dog from an animal shelter needs your very close vigilance for many weeks when he joins your family. You have no way of knowing what the dog's experiences have been and what sounds or incidents may reawaken terror or panic attacks. Sudden sounds or large vehicles passing by in the street, lawn mowers, bicycles, skateboards, or even baby carriages may trigger painful memories.

Be ready to cope with the situation and to calm your pet. It follows that the adult shelter dog must not have too much freedom and must never be placed in a situation that may lead to him being frightened. Fear in some dogs shows as an instinct to hide in dark corners or to run away. In others, it may cause a dog to attack. Get to know your adult dog as well as possible, as soon as possible.

OTHER COMMANDS

Enjoy playing with your dog, but you must decide when playtime is over. Your actions, your demeanor, the very tone of your voice when you are issuing commands must convey to a pet when playtime is over. Be consistent in each of these and your dog will soon learn what you want him to do.

Some dog trainers recommend putting the toys you play with away in a drawer until you want to play next time. If you do this, make sure that the dog always has a chewing toy of his own—a safe hard rubber toy or a nylon bone is best. Pups need to chew when they are getting their second set of teeth, a process that begins when they are about four months old and may continue throughout their first year.

In training your dog, consistency in following a command through is the important keynote. He must always do as you have said, but you must never lose your temper over the encounter. Go on being firm but kind until the dog has given up trying to defy you. Punishment is not appropriate, nor is shouting or violence. Young dogs are not so different from children in their attitudes to rebellion and compliance. Make it worth the dog's while to do as you wish. You should expect, as you would with a child, some attempts to test your firmness and resolution, but do not despair if at times you do not seem to be making a lot of progress.

Right: Rough play with a pet can teach dogs some bad lessons that may be hard to unlearn.

TIME ON THEIR OWN

It does a dog no harm to be ignored for short periods of time when you are busy. Your dog will enjoy your companionship and love the sound of your voice, but he will also need some peace and quiet, and this applies especially to a growing puppy. He should be allowed to sleep until he wakes naturally. When a puppy tires of play and goes into his crate, it is a good idea to leave him alone for a short time, perhaps for ten minutes at first, but extending for up to an hour. Eventually, you will probably have to leave your puppy alone all day.

If you start training the puppy to stay alone while you are in another room, you may soon hear the door being scratched and must let your pet know that such behavior is not allowed. However, don't be in too much of a hurry to go back to the dog—he will soon learn that he can gain your attention right away by destroying his surroundings.

When leaving a dog for an hour or two, always tidy the room first. Empty

OTHER ANIMALS

Do not leave your new dog or puppy with an older dog or a resident cat until the older animal has accepted the newcomer on his own terms. Cats should always be provided with a safe and comfortable place high up on top of a cupboard from which they can observe the antics of a puppy without feeling too much aggression.

the trash basket, remove any food; and make sure all the cupboards are securely fastened. Leave some toys in case the dog wakes. Many people leave a radio on, tuned in to a "talk" program, so that the sound of human voices provides companionship.

Make your "good-byes" very casual. You should not build up an emotional atmosphere between you and the dog—just go. You may want to think out a key phrase for departure, such as "Be a good dog, look after the house," but it is often better to say nothing at all. If your dog is destructive or barks and howls when you are out, the best strategy is to plan mock departures. Go out and close the door as if you have really left, and

then observe the dog's behavior. Tell him off in a severe tone of voice and then depart again, leaving your return a bit longer this time.

SOCIALIZATION

Socialization with all kinds of people and in a wide range of situations is crucial in developing a well-balanced companion animal.

◆ If possible, carry your puppy in your arms along a busy road so that he can hear and see traffic noises. Let passersby talk to the puppy. The prevailing view has always been that puppies should be kept within their own yards until they have completed the course of primary

PUPPY SOCIALIZATION

Your pup will need to learn how to act around other humans with their dogs. One of the best ways to do this is to enroll your pet in a puppy kindergarten class. You will have an opportunity to polish up your training skills and your dog will be around both other people and other dogs. This will be an environment where there are helpful experts who can answer any questions you may have.

vaccinations, probably at three-and-a-half to four months old. In Britain, the Guide Dogs for the Blind Association have pioneered the system of having puppies vaccinated for the first time at six weeks,

Below: Dogs need toys that they can feel are their own.

and then allowing them to be taken out and about during the most vital time for learning about the human world, which is between six and twelve weeks of age.

◆ As soon as the puppy or adult dog has complete confidence in your home, invite a range of people in to meet him, such as children, elderly people, or people of different ethnic groups. They all provide vital experiences for a puppy at his most impressionable age.

Above: Get your puppy used to being handled from an early age.

HANDLING THE PUPPY

Throughout your puppy's life you will need to be able to regularly check its eyes, ears, feet, and other body parts. Handle your puppy or dog as much as possible. Turn him on to his back and then pick him up; massage his legs; examine his toes; lift up his tail. Do all this gently and with consideration, and praise and reward afterwards, but make it clear that you can do anything reasonable and he must always submit. Establish mutual trust and then gradually extend the privilege to other adult family members.

TRAINING CLASSES

Reinforce the training you have given to your dog by joining a local training class. Experienced dog trainers can assist you in training your puppy, breaking any bad habits, and answering a great many questions about special circumstances that may arise. Many clubs also run competitive obedience training. Mixed breed dogs are often good at agility classes, so if you are fit yourself you may want to join in this cheerful activity. There are many display teams where mixed breeds are welcome, and where talents can range from absolute precision obedience to being the clown of the party—the one who specializes in doing it wrong! You can do so much more than just own a dog—have fun together and perhaps you will become stars of the canine world.

Above and right: Many dogs enjoy participating in agility classes where they can display their natural talents for jumping.

COMMON BEHAVIOR PROBLEMS

THE URGE TO WANDER

Many mixed breed dogs have an inherited tendency to be a free spirit and to wander. The best way to change this behavior is to make yourself, your home, and the yard the center of the dog's world, and the place where everything good happens in his life.

Neutering of both sexes undoubtedly helps. This removes the sexual urge to seek out mates.

FEAR BITING AND AGGRESSION

Ideally a dog should not be adopted from a shelter if he shows any signs of fear biting or aggression. Seek advice from the shelter staff. It may be that the problem goes much too deep for amateur retraining and some specialist help may be needed. Although we all want to see every disadvantaged dog make good, we have to accept that some dogs cannot be made safe for life with a human family.

THE ADULT DOG

B y the time your puppy grows into an adult, he should be housebroken and trained to be obedient. He should respond to your commands, and you should have got to know each other so well that you can both communicate effectively with each other. Your dog will have been assimilated into your home and will have become a much-loved family member and a loyal companion to you.

As well as feeding and exercising your dog on a daily basis, you should groom him regularly, bathe him occasionally, and keep a sharp eye on his general health to make sure that he stays fit and healthy.

DENTAL CARE

As your puppy comes to the end of his first year, check that all his puppy teeth have been shed, and that the permanent teeth are not coming through on top of the puppy set. Tooth extraction in dogs is relatively easy if your veterinarian advises that this is necessary.

The hard nylon toys are good for helping to keep the dog's teeth clean, and a hard biscuit as a treat also helps. Your

Above: You should examine your dog's mouth and teeth regularly. Get him accustomed to this from an early age so that he learns to trust your handling him. This will help to make visits to the veterinarian easier when he is older.

veterinarian will advise you if your dog's teeth need cleaning. You should regularly check your dog's mouth, teeth, and gums. Look for plaque, cavities, evidence of tooth decay, injuries, and foreign objects (wood splinters, bone fragments, etc.).

EYES

Always check your dog's eyes frequently, especially if you see any mucus discharge from the corner, if the eyes are held half closed, or the white part of the eye appears bloodshot. Some serious eye diseases resemble less urgent conditions on the surface. Do not use any medication without consulting your veterinarian.

NAILS

The majority of dogs will need to have their nails trimmed on a regular basis. Remove just the tip of nail. Some dogs will have dewclaws, a rudimentary nail, semicircular in shape, that grows roughly at the back of the leg. If this nail is growing around in a circle and threatens to penetrate the dog's leg, you should consult your veterinarian who will

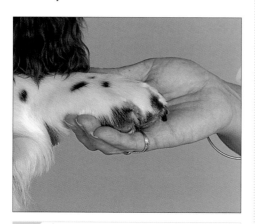

Above: Teach your dog to offer his feet to you to be examined.

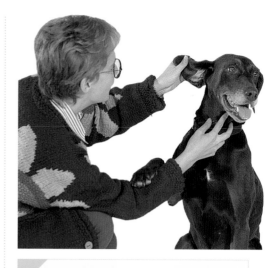

Above: Check inside your dog's ears for residue or infestation by parasites.

probably advise that the whole claw should be removed permanently.

EARS

Ears may be invaded by parasites. The signs of ear problems are persistent shaking of the head, scratching of the ears, holding one lower than the other, and/or a very pungent odor. Take a cotton ball and then gently wipe the ear inside; you may discover that you have removed quite a lot of residue.

Never attempt to use a cotton swab or in any way attempt to penetrate the depths of the ear. If the irritation and odor persist, take your dog to the veterinarian for a professional examination of his ears.

DIGESTIVE PROBLEMS

Keep a close watch on any episodes of vomiting and diarrhea. Refusal to eat is unimportant if it lasts only up to 48 hours—longer than that requires a professional opinion. Take a sample of the diarrhea as it may help the veterinarian in his diagnosis. Do not allow diarrhea to continue for several days without seeking veterinary advice as it can be a telltale sign of many serious medical conditions in a dog.

COUGHING

If your dog's cough sounds as though he has a bone stuck in his throat, it could be kennel cough, an airborne virus that is spread wherever dogs are gathered together and there is one infected dog. Telephone the veterinary clinic to say that you suspect kennel cough. It may be that the veterinarian will make some special arrangements to see you, as no one wants a coughing dog in the waiting room. Kennel cough can last a very long time so you must be patient and follow the full course of treatment. Do not take a coughing dog to a training class, a show, or any other canine gathering, and be aware that you can carry the virus on your clothing.

CHOKING

When your dog has a foreign body stuck in his throat, resulting in retching, an

WORMING

All dogs need a regular check for worms, as it is possible that the puppies may not have been wormed effectively and may carry a persistent burden. Consult the veterinarian where your pet can be weighed and prescribed a worm preparation.

inability to swallow, with drooling and saliva, and possible scratching at his mouth or throat, you must contact your veterinarian immediately (see page 118).

PARASITES

Fleas, mites, and ticks are a nuisance to all dogs. Having a dog scratching all the time is not pleasant and may lead to self-inflicted wounds that are difficult to heal. Everywhere your pet goes—inside, outside, even your car—can harbor fleas. Unless you treat each of these places, you won't eradicate the fleas. Ticks are always best removed manually before they become too engorged with blood. The veterinarian can show you how to remove a tick and you can do it for your dog thereafter. Do not neglect ticks—a large number on a small dog could cause anemia. Ticks are easily picked up in the country and in the woods. In fact, it may be possible that deer ticks carry Lyme disease, also known as borelliosis.

GROOMING

All dogs need to have dead hair, dust, and tangles removed from their coats and no dog can do this completely for himself. Even if your puppy has a very soft or shorthaired coat, get him accustomed to a regular grooming routine from the very beginning. This is another routine that is kindly but conveys to the puppy that he has to submit to what you want to do. It is best to groom a small puppy on your lap, but, later on, train your dog to stand on a convenient bench or table.

SMOOTH-COATED DOGS

◆ Smooth-coated dogs need to have dead hair removed quite frequently and they look all the better for this beauty routine.

◆ Smooth coats are groomed with a hound glove, a kind of mitt with an abrasive surface or wire bristles on one side and a velvet polisher on the other. In fact, you can remove a lot of dead hair just by stroking a smooth coat with a rubber-gloved hand, and then giving it a polish with a piece of pure silk.

◆ Talk to your dog all the time; always remember that the sound of your voice is a pleasure to him, and hand massage is very soothing.

◆ Complete your grooming by looking at the dog's feet. Some dogs seem to resent their feet being touched, so accustom your dog to offering his feet to you willingly. Check that the nails are not overlong; they should just touch the ground when the dog is standing. Some nails may be split or torn, so use nail clippers to take off any ragged pieces and finish by buffing them with an emery board.

LONG-COATED DOGS

◆ Long-coated dogs require more grooming. Depending on the dog's ancestry, the coat can be difficult to

GROOMING EQUIPMENT

Your local pet store or veterinarian will advise you on the tools most suited to grooming your dog. A hound glove is ideal for smooth-haired dogs, whereas a more traditional brush and comb work better on longhaired dogs.

Note: While you are grooming, always check for any swellings or lumps and report them to the veterinarian. They may be the beginnings of a malignant or benign tumor, so it is best to get any lump diagnosed early.

groom, or relatively easy. Some silky coats tend to clog into tangles very easily. These tangles are often found in the armpits or the groin. They can be quickly teased out but they will very soon mat again. The simplest thing is to clip out these tangles where they do not show.

◆ Go through the rest of the coat with a steel comb, taking out any burrs, leaves, and seeds. Surplus hair should be trimmed out from between the pads of the feet, and hair on the top of the feet may be trimmed short to help prevent any mud being brought into the house.

◆ Hair under the tail and near the genitals should be carefully trimmed off to avoid unpleasant odors. Clean around the anus with a pad of damp cotton. Be

sure to frequently and thoroughly remove any accumulated feces.

◆ If you have noticed your dog "scooting" on his behind, this may be caused by over-full, or even impacted, anal sacs—not worms. Take the dog to the veterinarian to have the anal sacs emptied.

◆ Give the coat a thorough brushing to get rid of dust and make it shine. Your dog will come to enjoy these grooming sessions.

Left: Teach your dog to stand on a table or a bench when you are grooming him.

BATHING YOUR DOG

Dogs should not require bathing very often—a couple of times a year is usually enough unless your dog makes a habit of rolling in unpleasant things. Small dogs are best bathed standing in the kitchen sink, on a pile of towels or a nonslip bath mat to prevent them slipping. A larger dog may have to be washed in the shower or outside in a tub in the backyard.

BATHING TIPS

◆ If you have a dog with many white areas in his coat, you might like to wash the white parts only without bathing the whole dog.

◆ Always use a dog shampoo, which is specially formulated for dogs.

◆ If you suspect that your dog has fleas, stand him on a sheet of white paper and comb the coat thoroughly. A lot of soot-like dust may drop down onto the paper. Pour a few drops of cold water onto this dust; if it turns red, your dog has fleas—the red coloring being the blood on which the fleas have fed. The dog must be bathed in either a good anti-parasitic shampoo or alternative product. The house, most especially the area where the dog lies and his bedding, should be treated with an

appropriate anti-parasitic spray. You can obtain these products from your veterinary clinic or pet store.

◆ Be careful to prevent soap from getting into the eyes.

◆ If you have a light-colored dog that needs bathing more often, it may be a

good idea to accustom him to being dried with a hair dryer. Take care not to have the dryer too hot and to keep it moving around the dog's body, not directing it for too long at any one area.

◆ Always dry the dog thoroughly, either with a hair dryer or by rubbing him well in a clean towel and then allowing him to dry off outside in the sun. Don't allow him to stay damp or to go to sleep in his crate before drying off.

STRIPPING AND TRIMMING YOUR DOG

Dogs that have terrier ancestry are likely to have wiry coats, which will require regular stripping to remove dead hair. Ask a dog groomer to show you how to do this with a stripping knife—a purpose-made tool with serrated edges. Alternatively, you may choose to have your dog professionally groomed several times a year.

DEAD HAIR AND SHEDDING

Really dense-coated Chow Chow or Spitz-type dogs need regular brushing, first the "wrong way" against the hair growth and then again to bring the hair back into place. Periodically these breeds, as well as Labrador and Old English Sheepdog crosses, will have a huge seasonal shedding, losing great quantities of their undercoat and topcoat.

Take your dog into the backyard and remove as much dead hair as possible.

EXERCISE

All dogs need a certain amount of exercise. Exercise, from the dog's point of view, is about developing and maintaining bodily skills, but it is also the equivalent of reading the local newspapers to find out what is going on and who or what is in the neighborhood.

However, to many owners, giving their dog free exercise can only happen when there is time to drive to a suitable open space. Letting a dog run free in an urban situation is dangerous for a wide range of reasons, including the danger from traffic, bicycles and pedestrians.

Find out if there is a park or a dog run near your home where your dog can run freely and safely off the lead.

Exercise is not only good for a dog's physical well-being but also its mental well-being. Many dogs will suffer from boredom or stress if they aren't allowed some regular physical activity each day. For some dogs, just walking with you is

Below: Dogs love to retrieve almost anything.

enough. Other dogs need a spirited romp.

Dogs need appropriate exercise and they may also need walks to places where they can relieve themselves. Perhaps no other area of urban dog ownership is as controversial as the way some owners neglect to pick up their pets' waste. No one wants to step in a pile of dog feces left behind because the dog's owner wouldn't clean it up. You should always carry plastic bags or some other method to pick up feces from off the street or wherever it is put. Not doing this is irresponsible and may make your pet and others unwelcome in your neighborhood.

PLAYTIME

Playing daily with your dog is equally important. Not only is it another means of exercising him but also a way of developing his mental skills and his bonding with the human family. Play is part of the fun of owning a dog, and it can take many forms. Indoor play focuses on "seek and find" skills, or catching a suitable

toy or tugging on a rope. You can reinforce your essential dominance by requiring the dog to give the toy to you— or by refusing to play at the moment when the dog requests your attention. If you play these games, make sure that you are always the winner, and call a halt by saying your keynote word or phrase, such as "that's enough."

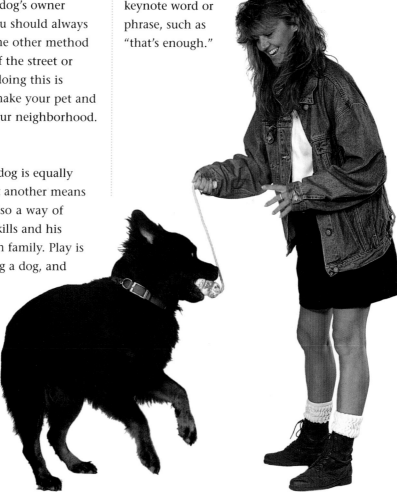

Right: Catching a moving object is one of the natural canine skills.

TRAVELING AND VACATIONS

You probably brought your new dog or puppy home in a car. This first journey is usually made with the dog being held securely on someone's lap but on subsequent journeys you should take measures to ensure your dog's safety.

CAR TRAVEL

Almost all dogs are likely to get carsick at first. The simplest way to get over this is to ignore the drooling and discomfort and clean up as best you can. Protect the upholstery as much as possible, and take the dog for several short journeys just to

get him accustomed to riding in the car. Pick a time before he is fed. It is rare for car sickness to persist, and when it does, it is probably because lots of remedies have been tried and an atmosphere of tension persists when a car ride is inevitable.

◆ The dog wants to be with you all the time and he will willingly jump into the car when you go out. Dogs have an excellent sense of balance so they have a natural ability to ride the roads.

◆ There are many accessories for canine car travel now available to make traveling safer for both the dog and the driver. An adaptation of the wire crate, which you use at home, can partition off the back of the car. Otherwise, there are canine seat belts on sale that will secure the dog on the back seat. Dogs should not be allowed to ride unrestrained or with their heads out of the car window.

◆ Never forget your dog's comfort in the car. Always carry some water and a bowl, and, in extremely hot weather, a sponge and wet towel are a practical way to cool down a dog which has become overheated.

◆ Never leave a dog in a car, even in slightly warm weather (over 65°F/18°C)—

Left: Many people enjoy going away on vacation with their dog.

carry a thermometer in the car and see how it heats up! Leaving windows open is of very little use as there is no current of air to cool the dog. A car very quickly becomes an oven, and every year some dogs die a cruel death through suffocation.

VACATIONS

Because your dog is part of your family, you will want to include him in your days out and your vacations. Pet lovers are finding an increasing number of hotels and campgrounds that will cater to them and their canine companion.

When you discover an accommodation that permits and welcomes dogs, it is wise to inquire in advance just what facilities will be available to you. Some hotels allow dogs into their grounds but require them to sleep in kennels, or in the owner's car overnight.

The general and understandable rule is that dogs are not permitted in restaurants or public rooms, and not in the bars of inns where food is served. Take care that what your dog does is not the excuse for banning dogs forever from that particular establishment.

Many camping sites or trailer parks require dogs to be tied up outside their owner's van. This is the way to bring out the worst behavior in any dog; examples include persistent barking, threatening people who approach too closely, and, almost inevitably, plotting every opportunity to escape. This is not much of

THE COUNTRY CODE

When out in the countryside, always keep your dog on a lead when you are near livestock. Even if he behaves impeccably, it is possible that cattle, sheep, and poultry may panic at the mere sight of him. Take special care to keep him on a lead when there are deer around—few dogs can resist the chase. All the training and domestication we can give is only a thin veneer over the basic wild dog. Think ahead for your pet and keep him out of trouble.

a holiday for either the dog or his owner.

TRAVELING BY AIR

It is possible for you to have your pet fly with you on many airlines. A small dog or small puppy could be carried on in a carrier, but larger pets have to travel in the baggage compartment. Traveling can be stressful on some dogs, and very young and very old pets are best left at home or in a boarding kennel.

Air travel for dogs is much safer than it once was, but you need to plan your flights so that you have few, if any, plane changes. Most airlines can rent you an approved airline carrier. You should also be at the airport early and always watch your pet being loaded on the same plane that you are to ride.

BOARDING KENNELS

It is not a bad thing to accustom your dog to going into a boarding kennel for one or two nights while he is still a puppy. Be certain that you alert the boarding kennel operator to any specific medications or health conditions that affect your pet. You should also make certain that your puppy or dog is to be given the same food that he has been eating at home.

Boarding kennels usually charge you by the day and have strict rules about the times during which dogs can be delivered and picked up. The best kennels get booked up very early for popular vacation periods so make arrangements for your dog as soon as you know you are going away. Be sure to ask which vaccinations are necessary and get them done at least two weeks before the dog goes into a boarding kennel.

THE ELDERLY DOG

Mixed breed dog owners are so fortunate—their dogs usually live longer than some of their pedigree cousins. However, even mixed breeds eventually show the inevitable signs of the aging process. So much more can be done for our dogs nowadays, so do not despair if your dog shows signs of illness.

◆ Lameness and pain on getting up from his bed are among the earliest signs that your dog has arthritis, a condition that is excruciatingly painful although movement sometimes eases the pain. There are medical treatments and even hip joint replacements, so consult your veterinarian.

◆ Elderly dogs may become partially or completely blind. They can manage extremely well in a familiar environment provided that all the furniture is kept in the same place. You will have to think ahead for your dog and protect him from any hazards.

◆ The same is true for the old dog who becomes deaf. Hand signals are quite helpful as is your continual watchfulness, especially when any household appliances are being used.

◆ Old dogs frequently seem confused when they wake from sleep; they appear not to know quite where they are. When outside, even in your own yard, the geriatric dog may move off surprisingly quickly albeit in completely the wrong direction.

◆ Care and consideration must be your watchwords. Elderly dogs appear to vary in health and capability from day to day. An aging dog may appreciate smaller, easily digested meals given more frequently, say, four times a day. When the teeth are no longer comfortable, soft food is easier for the dog to eat. Special treats, praise and affection can mean so much to both of you when your pet is approaching the end of his days.

◆ Incontinence can be a problem in old age, especially in spayed bitches. Once more, your veterinarian can help with medical treatment, and you can also save yourself trouble by protecting the dog's crate with a waterproof surface placed under a polyester fur rug.

◆ Best of all, old dogs love an old rug or bean bag to support their weary limbs. Smooth-coated dogs will be comforted by a dog sweater to cover the chest and haunches, and in drafty houses, the sweater may be necessary, even indoors; but take it off as often as you can to allow air to the skin.

◆ Keep your elderly pet clean by wiping his mouth, face, and whiskers after eating, and removing any mucus from the eyes with damp cotton. Never hesitate to consult your veterinarian about any of your dog's disabilities. The fear that you will be told that putting him to sleep is the answer should be banished from your mind because it is no longer true. Veterinarians are very skilled and are eager to keep an enduring pet relationship going for as long as both the owner and the dog benefit and are happy together.

HEALTH AND FIRST AID

SIGNS OF A HEALTHY DOG

A happy, healthy dog wags his tail and is always pleased to see you.

◆ He is bright and alert.

◆ He has a good appetite.

◆ He is eager to go for a walk and does not limp.

◆ His eyes are bright and free of any discharge.

◆ His teeth are clean and his breath is not unpleasant.

◆ There should be no discharge from the nostrils. Neither the temperature nor moisture of the tip of the nose are reliable indicators of health in a dog.

◆ The ears should have no residue or odor and should be pain-free.

◆ He should breathe through the nose when resting; through the mouth when excited or hot.

◆ He scratches occasionally, but not persistently.

◆ He produces a solid bowel movement (with no traces of mucus or blood) once or twice a day.

◆ He has no discharges or unpleasant smells from the anus or genitals.

DIET

Dogs need some basic nutrients in their diet, as supplied by quality dog foods:

◆ **Protein** from meat, fish, eggs or milk for growth and repair of body tissues.

◆ **Carbohydrates** from cereal starches and root vegetables for energy and heat.

◆ **Fat** from dairy produce, meat and oils for energy, palatability, and fat-soluble vitamins.

◆ **Water, vitamins, and minerals.**

It is not easy to put together a satisfactory diet at home, as all these elements need to be present in the right proportions and correct quantities to take into account the dog's size, age, and activity.

For the majority of owners, it is better to feed a pre-prepared diet, of which there is a bewildering variety available in pet stores and supermarkets, including:

◆ Canned   ◆ Semimoist

◆ Complete dry   ◆ Frozen

The best advice on how to select a particular brand is to choose one recommended for your type of dog and his age that suits your dog, is palatable and does not cause digestive upset or any

SPECIAL DIETS

A number of manufacturers now make special diets for the various stages of a dog's life, to take account of their changing nutritional requirements. These include the following:
♦ Puppies from weaning to four months who should be fed four meals per day.
♦ Puppies from four to five months who need three meals per day.
♦ Puppies from five to six months on two meals per day.
♦ Puppies and adults from six months onward on one or two meals a day.
♦ Growing, working, pregnant, or lactating dogs who need to eat more than normal adults.
♦ Older dogs who generally need less protein.
♦ Overweight dogs who need fewer calories.
♦ Sick dogs with special dietary needs.
Note: Ask your veterinarian's advice if your dog fits into any of these categories.

other health problems, fits your budget and is regularly available locally.

♦ PRESCRIPTION DIETS
There is also an increasing range of diets available on veterinary prescription for the treatment and management of certain diseases, such as heart disease, kidney or liver failure, and allergies.

♦ SCRAPS AND SUPPLEMENTS
If you choose to give your dog table scraps, they should make up no more than 10 percent of the dog's total diet. Vitamin and mineral supplements are not normally necessary when feeding commercial dog foods except in pregnancy and lactation, and should be given only on veterinary advice.

♦ BONES
Dogs often enjoy chewing bones, and although these may keep them occupied for some time, they can also cause problems, such as broken teeth, choking, or bowel obstructions. There are many different types of dog chews on the market that are far more trouble-free, and should be given in preference to bones.

EXERCISE

All dogs need exercise, but how much and how often depends on the size and build of your dog. He needs to be let out to urinate and defecate, to exercise his muscles, to meet and play with other dogs, and to alleviate boredom. Walking on the lead is good discipline, but free exercise in a safe place may be appropriate in your area. Teach your dog to play with toys, such as ropes, balls, and tugs.

You should limit the exercise for your dog if he has breathing problems, a heart condition, is lame, has had a recent injury, or has a digestive problem. When it is hot, go out early in the morning or wait until evening to avoid the possibility of heatstroke (see Heatstroke, page 122).

DAILY CARE

As part of the daily care of your dog, you should briefly check the following.

◆ TEETH
Regular tooth brushing, using a special dog toothbrush and a dog toothpaste (special flavors—they don't like mint!) will discourage the build up of deposits of tartar on the teeth, keeping the dog's teeth healthy and his breath fresh. Start gently to get him used to the idea; handle his mouth, lift his lips, and run your finger along the outside of his teeth. Once he is used to this, slowly insert the brush along the side of the mouth, and gently brush up and down and along the teeth. You can always ask your veterinarian for a dental check up just to make sure that everything is in order.

TEETH AND JAWS

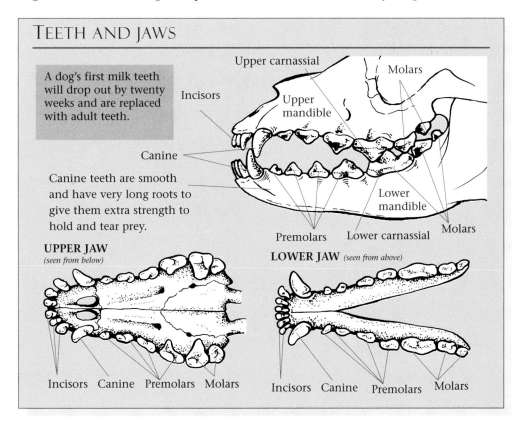

A dog's first milk teeth will drop out by twenty weeks and are replaced with adult teeth.

Incisors

Upper carnassial

Molars

Upper mandible

Canine

Canine teeth are smooth and have very long roots to give them extra strength to hold and tear prey.

Lower mandible

Premolars   Lower carnassial   Molars

UPPER JAW *(seen from below)*

LOWER JAW *(seen from above)*

Incisors Canine Premolars Molars

Incisors Canine Premolars Molars

◆ EYES

The eyes should be bright and clear, with no discharge or redness. You can check your dog's vision by throwing a cottonball in front of him, and noting whether he is able to follow it. The cornea should be clear, not cloudy, and the third eyelid well down in the corner. Both eyes should be open the same amount and appear the same size: any difference may be due to pain or disease, and should be checked.

◆ EARS

Normal ears have just a trace of light brown wax, and little or no odor. If your dog's ears are excessively hairy, this may encourage the build up of wax, and reduce healthy air circulation to the ear canal, so keep the hair well trimmed. A powerful odor, discharge, scratching at the ears, or pain on touching them are all signs of ear infection, and should be dealt with immediately by your veterinarian.

◆ NOSE

There are many theories about whether dogs' noses should be warm, cool, moist, or dry, but these are not reliable indicators of health or disease. Normal noses simply do vary a lot. What you are looking out

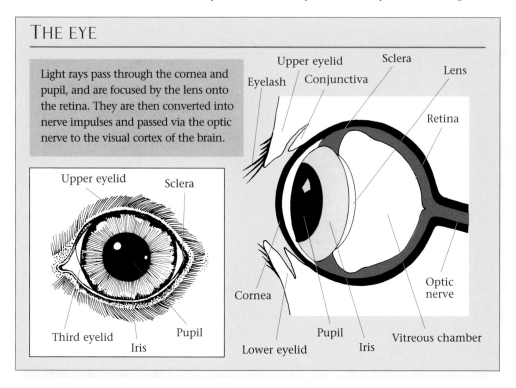

THE EYE

Light rays pass through the cornea and pupil, and are focused by the lens onto the retina. They are then converted into nerve impulses and passed via the optic nerve to the visual cortex of the brain.

Upper eyelid

Sclera

Upper eyelid   Sclera   Lens

Eyelash   Conjunctiva

Retina

Cornea

Third eyelid   Pupil

Iris

Lower eyelid   Pupil   Iris   Optic nerve

Vitreous chamber

for are any signs of a discharge, any change in shape, color, sneezing, ulcers, or thickening of the nasal pad.

◆ **FEET**
"Lame is pain," so any limping should be investigated by your veterinarian, but a good daily check at home is a sensible routine, particularly if your dog is sensitive about having his feet touched. Make a game of it until he doesn't mind anymore. Check the length of his nails and the skin between the pads; it should be pale pink, with no redness or swellings. Longhaired dogs benefit from having the hair between the toes and pads trimmed short; this prevents mats forming and discourages grass seeds from working their way into the skin of the foot.

◆ **URINE AND FECES**
There is no need to become obsessed here, but just check now and again on the frequency of defecation, that the feces are of firm, even consistency and dark brown in color, with no signs of mucus, blood, or foreign material, such as cloth or plastic. If your dog has any diarrhea, it is better to call the veterinarian for advice. Dogs vary enormously in the number of times they stop to pass urine; very frequent urination may just be territory marking. The urine should be pale yellow. If you see your dog trying to urinate, but without success—staying in

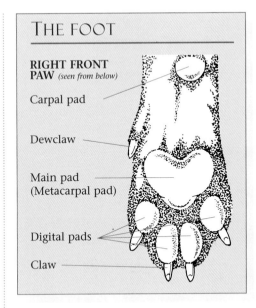

THE FOOT

RIGHT FRONT PAW *(seen from below)*

Carpal pad

Dewclaw

Main pad
(Metacarpal pad)

Digital pads

Claw

position but not producing anything—ask your veterinarian to have a look.

◆ **GROOMING**
Regular combing with a metal comb, or brushing, helps remove any loose dead hair, and prevents mats forming. Wiry coats benefit from stripping out every three to four months, and curly-coated dogs may need to be clipped to prevent the coat from growing too long.

A very fine-tooth metal comb will pick up any fleas or flea residue (small brown flakes), and so tell you when you need to repeat any flea treatments. Dogs may be bathed, but only use a mild dog shampoo and follow veterinary advice so as not to dry out the coat and skin.

PERIODIC HEALTH CARE

◆ VACCINATION

Dogs can now be vaccinated against many of the important infectious diseases: rabies, distemper, adenovirus 1 and 2, leptospirosis and parvovirus. Puppies should be vaccinated for the first time at eight to nine weeks old or as advised by your veterinarian who knows the local risks, with a second injection at around twelve weeks, and then yearly boosters thereafter.

Note: A kennel cough vaccine is also available, giving good protection within five days. It lasts for six to ten months.

◆ WORMING

Many puppies are born infected with roundworms, and can pick up further infections from their environment in their first three months of life. Feces from puppies less than six months old and from pregnant bitches or those around the time of their season should be picked up and disposed of, as they are likely to contain worm eggs. After two to three weeks outside the dog, these eggs become infective, both for dogs and children (see Zoonoses, page 107).

◆ Worm all puppies every two weeks from two weeks old up until they are twelve weeks of age.

◆ Worm all adult dogs at least twice yearly and during pregnancy.

◆ Tapeworms cannot be passed directly from dog to dog in one species: the flea is part of its life cycle. All dogs should be treated for tapeworms at least twice yearly.

◆ Signs of worm infestation include licking at the anus, occasional diarrhea and weight loss, and pot belly in puppies.

◆ NEUTERING, STERILIZATION, SPAYING, AND CASTRATION

Dogs are usually neutered when they are physically mature, typically from six months onward. However, new surgical methods allow routine neutering of dogs as young as eight weeks old.

◆ **For female dogs** the standard neutering operation is an ovariohysterectomy, best performed before her first heat. This involves removing both the ovaries and the body of the uterus or womb. It

COMMON WORMS

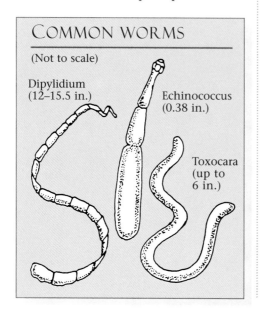

(Not to scale)

Dipylidium (12–15.5 in.)

Echinococcus (0.38 in.)

Toxocara (up to 6 in.)

therefore will prevent a bitch from coming into season again, stopping all the unwanted attentions of local male dogs, avoiding the problems of bleeding from the vulva during the season, and preventing any possibility of future pregnancies or the development of a womb infection—pyometra—in later life. It also dramatically reduces the likelihood of your dog developing mammary cancer.

Hormonal control of your bitch's seasons is also possible, but not without side effects, and the long-term expense can be considerable. Check your dog's mammary glands after each season for signs of milk production or any swellings.

◆ **In male dogs**, castration involves the complete removal of both testicles. These are the main source of male sex hormones, so castration of a younger dog is likely to reduce his desire to stray or wander off in search of bitches in season, and may help to control his "mounting," territory marking with urine or any aggressive behavior he may develop. Certain diseases, for example, cancer of the prostate gland or hormonally controlled tumors, may also benefit from castration.

◆ **FLEA CONTROL**

The main source of new flea infestation for dogs is from fleas newly hatched from the breeding grounds in your house, not from other animals. Adult fleas spend their entire three-week life on an animal,

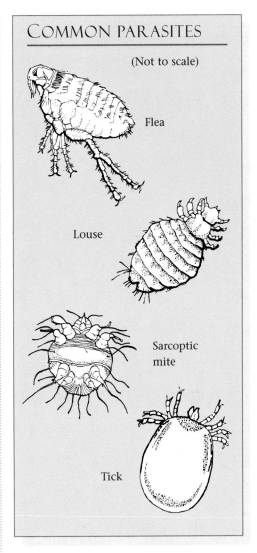

COMMON PARASITES

(Not to scale)

Flea

Louse

Sarcoptic mite

Tick

feeding on their blood. Each adult flea lays around twenty eggs a day: these 400 flea eggs drop off the animal onto the dog's bedding or a domestic carpet, and, after hatching, develop into larvae and then pupae and, finally, more adults,

TICK REMOVAL

Never simply pull a tick off your dog. Doing so may leave part of the tick in your dog's skin to cause irritation and possible infection. Ask your veterinarian to remove the tick and to show you how to do it safely.

who each may lay up to 400 more eggs. The whole process may take a few weeks or as long as a year.

In order to have effective flea control on your dog, it is very important to stop the build up of a developing flea population in your house. There are three main types of flea control:

1. External treatment for the dog that kills adult fleas currently present (sprays, powders, shampoos, drops for the coat)

2. Treatment for the home environment that kills developing fleas (mostly sprays)

3. A prescription medicine, available only from your veterinary clinic, given to your dog in his food each month, that stops the fleas from reproducing

◆ IDENTIFICATION

It is very wise for your dog to wear a collar and external identification, such as an engraved disk or dog tag, whenever he goes out, so make sure that he always wears his. It is now possible to have a microchip with the dog's identification number on it placed under his skin—this is relatively painless and can be done while you wait at the veterinary clinic. A microchip reader, as used by animal shelters, veterinary clinics, and humane societies all over the country, will rapidly identify your dog and allow you to be reunited should he ever get lost!

◆ NAIL CLIPPING

Regular exercise on a hard surface, such as pavements and hard ground, will normally keep your dog's nails at the correct length. Check regularly for overgrowth and for any signs of discharge around the base of the nail. Trim nails where necessary, avoiding the sensitive tissue (the quick). Ask your veterinarian for guidance on this.

HEALTH PROBLEMS OF MIXED BREED DOGS

Mixed breed dogs are the product of a mix of genetic material. They are not predisposed to the wide range of inherited and congenital problems that plague many pedigree breeds which have been selected for their looks or specific aspects of their performance. However, mixed breeds are susceptible to infectious disease and to the aging process.

DISEASES AND ILLNESSES

RESPIRATORY DISEASES

When a dog breathes in, air containing
oxygen is drawn through the nose or
mouth, down the windpipe (trachea) and
into the lungs through the bronchi.
Relaxation of the breathing muscles pushes
the waste air back out again.

◆ SIGNS AND CAUSES

The main signs of respiratory disease are
coughing, difficulty in breathing, nasal
discharge, or sneezing due to infection,
inflammation, and irritation, or an
accumulation of fluid or discharges in the
respiratory system. Inflammation of the

lung tissue is called pneumonia; in the
bronchial tubes (bronchitis); the windpipe
(tracheitis); or in the nose (rhinitis).

Respiratory disease may be caused by
bacterial, viral, or parasitic infections,
heart or circulatory system disease, or
allergies, and certain types of cancer may
spread (metastasize) from a primary site
elsewhere to the lungs. Inhalation of food
or other foreign material, buildup of fluid
around the lungs, excessive heat or the
malfunctioning of the larynx or trachea
may also cause signs of respiratory
disease. Your veterinarian will examine
your dog's respiratory system using a

THE RESPIRATORY SYSTEM

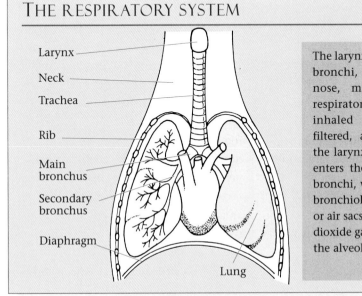

Larynx

Neck

Trachea

Rib

Main
bronchus

Secondary
bronchus

Diaphragm

Lung

The larynx, trachea, lungs, and
bronchi, together with the
nose, make up the dog's
respiratory system. Air is
inhaled through the nose,
filtered, and passed through
the larynx into the trachea. It
enters the lungs through the
bronchi, which subdivide into
bronchioles and end in alveoli,
or air sacs. Oxygen and carbon
dioxide gases are exchanged in
the alveoli.

stethoscope, and then may want to take chest X rays, use an endoscope to look down the dog's windpipe, or take samples of the discharges for laboratory analysis.

◆ KENNEL COUGH (Parainfluenza)
(See Infectious Diseases, below.)

◆ CARDIAC COUGH
(See Heart and Circulation, page 107.)

INFECTIOUS DISEASES

◆ PARVOVIRUS
This is a very contagious virus infection, causing heart muscle disease in puppies, and hemorrhagic gastroenteritis in older dogs. Affected animals can succumb very rapidly, and are in urgent need of veterinary care. All puppies should be vaccinated from eight to nine weeks old.

◆ DISTEMPER
This is a virus infection affecting the respiratory, digestive, and nervous systems. The incubation period is from two to seven days. Distemper causes a high temperature, nasal and ocular discharges, coughing, vomiting, and diarrhea, progressing to fits and death. Treatment depends on the stage of the disease, and is mainly symptomatic, but it may include broad-spectrum antibiotics and anti-convulsants if the nervous system is involved. Effective vaccines are available.

◆ VIRAL HEPATITIS
A serious and highly contagious viral infection, this primarily affects the liver,

with an incubation period of five to fifteen days. It is most common in young dogs. Signs of infection include vomiting, diarrhea, fever, abdominal pain, prostration, and death. These dogs are in urgent need of veterinary care, but treatment is mainly symptomatic, and may not be successful. This disease can be prevented simply by vaccination.

◆ RESPIRATORY ADENOVIRUS
This virus infection is related to the canine hepatitis virus. It causes a localized respiratory infection.

◆ LEPTOSPIROSIS
This is a bacterial infection carried by rats; it is present in some stagnant ponds. It affects the dog's liver or kidneys. The incubation period is from five to fifteen days. It causes fever, thirst, vomiting, jaundice, and diarrhea, progressing to profound depression and death. Prompt and intensive antibiotic and intravenous fluid treatment can be lifesaving. This disease is transmissible to humans.

◆ KENNEL COUGH (Parainfluenza)
This is a highly contagious mixed bacterial (Bordetella) and viral infection of the upper respiratory system. It has an incubation period of five to ten days. Infection is rarely severe, but may be distressing for the dog and owner. It is generally self-limiting in two to three weeks.

◆ SALMONELLOSIS
A relatively rare cause of bacterial enteritis in dogs, this can be a potential hazard to

humans in contact (see Zoonoses, below).

◆ CAMPYLOBACTER

This causes a profuse bacterial diarrhea, and is found in up to 10 percent of dogs with enteritis. It can be contagious to people.

◆ RABIES

This is a virus disease of the central nervous system, spread by saliva (mostly from bites), and affecting all mammals. It is still prevalent in many parts of the U.S. It has a long incubation period of up to ten months, during which time no symptoms are seen, but the virus may be present in the dog's saliva during the last few days or weeks. Marked behavioral changes, either the "furious" or "dumb" forms, lead to inevitable death as the brain becomes affected. Modern vaccines provide a good level of protection.

◆ ZOONOSES

Zoonoses are animal diseases that can also be caught by humans. Fortunately these are relatively rare. They include:

◆ **Roundworms** (toxoacara visceral larva migrans), which can cause eye problems in children

◆ **Ringworm**, a fungal skin infection that may be disfiguring

◆ **Fleas and ticks**

◆ **A type of tapeworm** (echinococcus hydatid cysts in the liver or brain)

◆ **Leptospirosis**, a liver and kidney infection

◆ **Scabies**, an irritant rash caused by the sarcoptic mange mite

SENSIBLE PRECAUTIONS

◆ Vaccinate your dog against any contagious diseases.
◆ Always wash your hands after handling your dog.
◆ Always use separate food bowls and implements for dogs and people.
◆ Worm your dog at least twice a year.
◆ Clear up your dog's feces, using a "poop scoop," both in your yard and in public.
◆ Do not let your dog lick your children's faces.
◆ Wash your dog's bedding frequently.
◆ Routinely treat your dog for fleas and other external parasites.
◆ Have your dog's health regularly checked by your veterinarian.
◆ Keep your dog's vaccinations up to date.

◆ **Salmonella and campylobacter** (gastroenteritis)
◆ **Giardiasis, tuberculosis, brucellosis, chlamydia, pasteurella, tetanus, and allergies**

HEART AND CIRCULATION DISEASES

Contractions of the heart muscle pump blood through a system of valves, sending it, under pressure, around the body. The blood takes oxygen and nutrients to the body's cells, and carries away their waste products. For the system to work well, the heart muscle has to pump regularly, the valves must not leak, and the blood vessels must remain elastic.

◆ SIGNS OF DISEASE

The signs of heart or circulatory disease that develops with advancing age— commonly a progressive failure of the valves to close properly or of the muscle to contract efficiently—are weakness and a reduced ability to exercise, breathing difficulty, and coughing. Internal bleeding, liver disease, overwhelming infections, or tumors can also cause signs of circulatory disease.

◆ DIAGNOSIS

Your veterinarian will initially feel your dog's pulse, then listen to the rhythm and rate of the heart and to the sounds of the heart valves with a stethoscope. More detailed investigation may involve taking X rays of the chest, taking electrical measurements or an ultrasound scan to see a moving image of the heart.

◆ TREATMENT

Excess fluid buildup may be cleared by the use of diuretics, which stimulate fluid loss through the kidneys, and by reducing the sodium (salt) content of the diet. Other drugs modify the heart's output and the blood pressure.

SECTION OF THE HEART

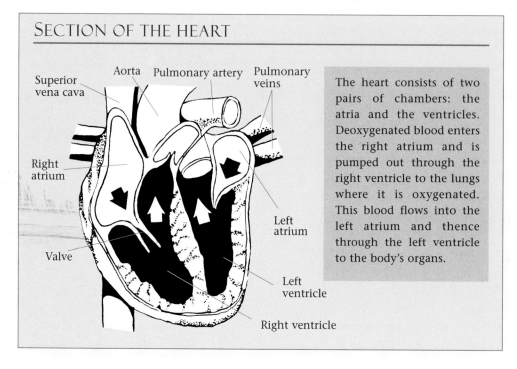

The heart consists of two pairs of chambers: the atria and the ventricles. Deoxygenated blood enters the right atrium and is pumped out through the right ventricle to the lungs where it is oxygenated. This blood flows into the left atrium and thence through the left ventricle to the body's organs.

THE DIGESTIVE SYSTEM

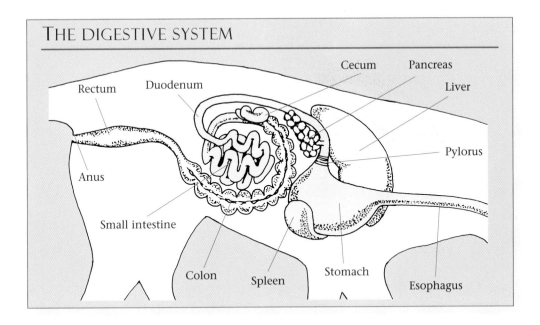

Cecum
Pancreas
Rectum
Duodenum
Liver
Pylorus
Anus
Small intestine
Colon
Spleen
Stomach
Esophagus

DIGESTIVE SYSTEM DISEASES

The teeth are used to tear and grind food, the stomach further breaks it down, and true digestion takes place in the small intestine. The large intestine is mainly concerned with the reabsorption of fluid, and the rectum stores feces before they are passed at intervals through the anus.

◆ Digestive system diseases include those of abnormal motility of the gut, abnormal secretion of digestive enzymes, the inflammation of the gut wall, and the malfunction of the pancreas and liver.

◆ SIGNS OF DISEASE
The signs of disease may include vomiting, diarrhea, or constipation, changes in appetite, or weight loss.

◆ DIAGNOSIS
Your veterinarian will ask you questions about the frequency, quantity, color, and consistency of any vomit or diarrhea passed, and about changes in appetite and recent diet, and may need to take a blood or stool sample from your dog.

◆ TREATMENT
This may involve changes in diet, or some treatment with antibiotics, anti-inflammatories, or drugs that affect the motility of the gut (see Diarrhea, page 120, Vomiting, page 126).

DENTAL DISEASE

A dog's teeth are used for tearing and chewing food, for biting, and, when bared,

SECTION OF A TOOTH

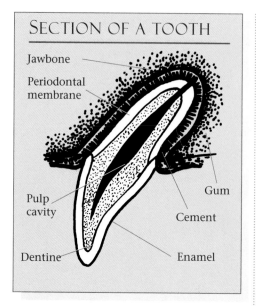

Jawbone

Periodontal membrane

Pulp cavity

Dentine

Gum

Cement

Enamel

for signaling aggression. The primary teeth start to fall out at four to five months of age, but they are frequently swallowed, so may not be noticed.

◆ **SIGNS OF DISEASE**

On modern pre-prepared diets, the teeth are often underused, and large deposits of dental tartar can build up. This may be associated with varying degrees of periodontal disease: bacterial infection, gum recession, salivation, pain, bleeding, and halitosis.

◆ **TREATMENT**

This involves breaking off the tartar, polishing the teeth to slow down the deposition of new tartar, and a long-term program of toothbrushing carried out by the dog's owner at home.

LIVER DISEASES

The liver plays a major role in the metabolism of carbohydrates, proteins, fats, and vitamins. It breaks down a wide variety of toxic products in the blood and produces bile (essential for the digestion of fats in the gut).

Liver disease may be rapid in onset (e.g., virus hepatitis, poisoning, or trauma) or slowly developing (chronic hepatitis, cirrhosis, or tumors).

◆ **SIGNS OF DISEASE**

These vary widely, from liver swelling or shrinkage, jaundice (yellowing), fluid accumulation in the abdomen, weight loss and changes in the color of the feces, to effects on the nervous system.

◆ **DIAGNOSIS**

Veterinary investigation will generally involve blood tests, X rays or ultrasound examination, taking a urine sample, or a liver biopsy.

◆ **TREATMENT**

This is mainly through careful control of the dog's diet and medication.

SKIN DISEASES

The skin is a layer of tissue that covers and protects the dog's body and collects sensory information about the external environment. Skin disease is very common in dogs, and may affect all areas, including the feet, ears, and any skin folds.

◆ **SIGNS OF DISEASE**

These are commonly seen as itching, scratching, redness, discharges from the skin surface, skin thickening, scaling, change in hair color or hair loss.

◆ **CAUSES**

The causes are numerous, but include:

◆ Parasites (fleas, ticks, mites, lice)

◆ Allergies to parasites, inhaled dust, and pollens, food, or chemical products

◆ Bacterial, viral, or fungal infections

◆ Hormonal imbalances, poor diet, immune disorders

◆ Skin warts, tumors, blocked anal glands, and wax-filled ears may all cause local distress and lead to self-trauma and local infection.

◆ **DIAGNOSIS**

Your veterinarian will probably ask you

STRUCTURE OF THE SKIN

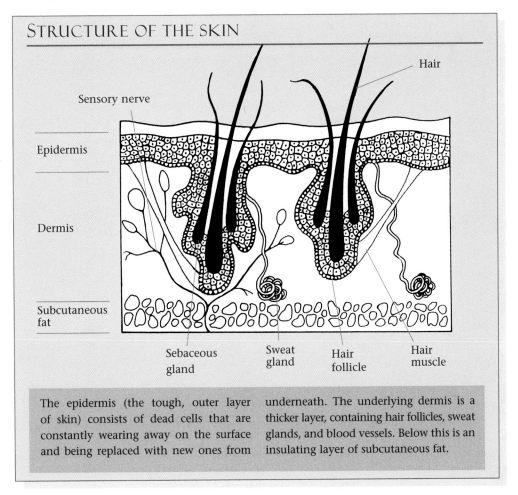

Sensory nerve

Hair

Epidermis

Dermis

Subcutaneous fat

Sebaceous gland

Sweat gland

Hair follicle

Hair muscle

The epidermis (the tough, outer layer of skin) consists of dead cells that are constantly wearing away on the surface and being replaced with new ones from underneath. The underlying dermis is a thicker layer, containing hair follicles, sweat glands, and blood vessels. Below this is an insulating layer of subcutaneous fat.

numerous questions about your dog's history, lifestyle, contacts, and diet, and in a more complex case may need to take samples of coat brushings, skin scrapings, blood samples, and bacteriological swabs.

◆ **TREATMENT**

The aim is to eliminate the cause of disease. Persistent cases, particularly those involving allergies, may need long-term treatment with steroid drugs.

EAR DISEASE

The ears are made up of four main parts: the outer flap, the external canal (down to the eardrum), the middle ear, and the inner ear (hearing and balance). The common ear diseases are mostly due to infection with bacteria, yeasts, or ear mites; the presence of foreign bodies, such as grass seeds; or excess hair and wax. The lining of the ear canal is skin, so any disease affecting the skin can also affect the ear canal itself.

◆ **SIGNS OF DISEASE**

These include head shaking, scratching, a smell or discharge from the ear, and pain.

◆ **DIAGNOSIS**

An otoscope is used to look down into the ear (this might be painful if the ear is very inflamed) and swabs may be taken for analysis when there is infection.

◆ **TREATMENT**

This is to clear the accumulated discharge and eliminate the infection, but in severe

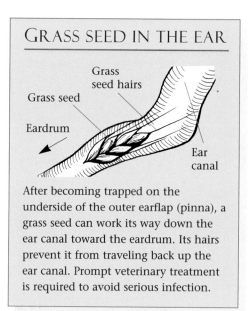

GRASS SEED IN THE EAR

Grass seed hairs

Grass seed

Eardrum

Ear canal

After becoming trapped on the underside of the outer earflap (pinna), a grass seed can work its way down the ear canal toward the eardrum. Its hairs prevent it from traveling back up the ear canal. Prompt veterinary treatment is required to avoid serious infection.

cases may involve surgery to improve the air circulation to the ear canal, or to remove chronically infected tissue.

Note: Repeated scratching and shaking of the head can damage the blood vessels in the earflap, leading to the formation of a large blood blister, an aural hematoma, in the earflap. This will need surgical drainage. Consult your veterinarian.

EYE DISEASE

Whereas pedigree dogs are susceptible to a wide range of inherited structural eye diseases, the problems affecting mixed breed dogs are more due to infection and injury.

◆ **SIGNS OF EYE DISEASE**

These include a discharge (clear or pus),

squinting (eye half closed), rubbing at the eye, or protrusion of the third eyelid. Trauma to the transparent cornea on the front of the eye may lead to a corneal ulcer, which is painful for the dog and, if untreated, may progress to a ruptured eye.

◆ **Conjunctivitis** is inflammation of the tissues around the eye, commonly due to bacterial infection.

◆ **Cataracts** As the lens ages, or as a result of diseases such as diabetes, it may become increasingly opaque, with the dog's vision deteriorating. In severe cases, the lens may dislocate from its normal position; surgery may be possible to remove a cataractous lens.

◆ **Trauma** Severe trauma, for example, after a road accident, may force the eye out of its socket. Damage to the cornea may include punctures or tears. Both these conditions need urgent veterinary attention (see Eye Prolapse, page 121).

URINARY SYSTEM DISEASE

Circulating blood passes through the kidneys, which filter out waste products and excess water. The urine produced passes down the ureters to the bladder, where it is stored until being passed via the urethra to the exterior. Kidney failure leads to the build up of waste products in the bloodstream.

◆ **SIGNS OF DISEASE**
Kidney disease in a dog may cause the accumulation of waste products in the

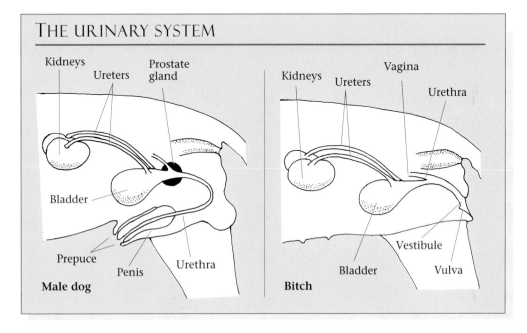

THE URINARY SYSTEM

Kidneys
Ureters
Prostate gland
Bladder
Prepuce
Penis
Urethra
Male dog

Kidneys
Ureters
Vagina
Urethra
Vestibule
Bladder
Vulva
Bitch

body (uremia), due to an inability to filter blood, whereas bladder diseases may show up as an increased frequency of urination, pain on urination or the presence of blood or pus in the urine. Abnormally high levels of various salts in the urine can lead to the formation of crystals and stones; these may eventually cause a urinary blockage. Urinary obstruction is painful and distressing. It is most common in male dogs. If your dog repeatedly tries to pass urine but cannot, see your veterinarian. Cystitis is common in bitches—when they strain to pass urine, a few drops are passed. Laboratory analysis of urine and blood samples will be part of the normal investigation.

Dogs may also suffer from incontinence, due to immaturity, nerve injury, or old age; some of these cases are now treatable. You should visit your veterinarian if your dog has any significant changes in his normal pattern of drinking or urination.

REPRODUCTIVE ORGANS

The testes in the scrotum produce sperm for the male dog, and the ovaries in the bitch's abdomen produce eggs. Normal mating involves the introduction of sperm into the female vagina via the penis. In the bitch, the muscles of the vagina contract toward the end of mating, retaining the penis in the vagina, and leading to what is called a "tie."

THE REPRODUCTIVE SYSTEM

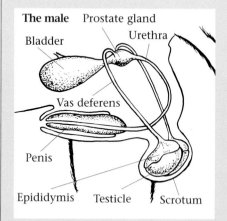

The male   Prostate gland

Bladder   Urethra

Vas deferens

Penis

Epididymis   Testicle   Scrotum

Sperm and testosterone are produced in the male dog's testicles. Sperm pass into the epididymis for storage, thence via the vas deferens during mating.

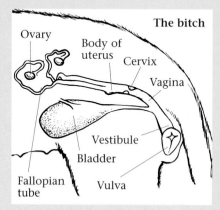

The bitch

Ovary   Body of uterus   Cervix

Vagina

Vestibule

Fallopian tube   Bladder   Vulva

Eggs are produced in the ovaries and enter the uterus through the fallopian tubes. During the heat period, they can be fertilized by sperm.

◆ It is not unusual for a male dog to have a discharge from the sheath, but if associated with repeated licking, a heavy discharge or noticeable odor, there may be infection present. Unequal swellings in the testicles may be due to infection or tumors. Enlargement of the prostate gland may cause difficulty urinating.

◆ Signs of a pyometra in a bitch include an increase in thirst, a reduction in appetite, lethargy, and a purulent vaginal discharge, typically around one month after a season.

◆ **FALSE PREGNANCY**
After a normal season, some dogs will show signs of a false pregnancy, for example, behavior changes, milk production, bed making, carrying shoes or other small objects around the house. The dog hormonally "thinks" that she is pregnant, despite not having been mated. These signs mostly pass off without treatment, but are another argument for spaying. Inflammation and infection of the mammary glands are called mastitis, and warrants veterinary attention.

NERVOUS SYSTEM DISEASE

Sensory information from internal and external sense organs, such as the ears, eyes, and nose, is sent along the nerves to the central nervous system in the dog's spinal cord and brain, which are heavily protected by the skull and the spine. However, the nervous system is very susceptible to injury, whether from blunt trauma (e.g., road accidents), infection (e.g., canine distemper) or poisoning.

◆ **SIGNS OF NERVOUS SYSTEM DISEASE**
These are varied and include dullness or depression, pain, increased excitability, twitching, or full-blown convulsions. All changes in the state of consciousness of your dog will warrant a full veterinary examination (see Convulsions (Fits), page 120).

THE MUSCULOSKELETAL SYSTEM

The skeletal system is made up of the bones, muscles, and joints. Bones have a calcified protein structure, and are strong but brittle; hence, they break fairly easily. At the joints, the ends of the bones are covered with a low-friction, smooth cartilage surface and encased in a sac of sticky fluid—joint fluid—to lubricate them. A system of muscles is attached to the skeleton to move the limbs as required.

◆ **ARTHRITIS**
This is a degenerative inflammation of the joints, commonly in response to age, trauma, or infection. The signs are pain, lameness, and joint swelling. Treatment depends on the cause, but often involves the long-term use of anti-inflammatory drugs (see Broken Bones (Fractures), page 117, Dislocation, page 120).

THE SKELETON

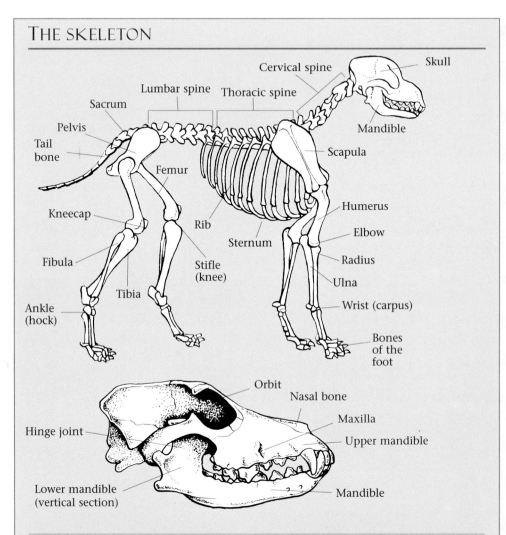

Cervical spine

Skull

Lumbar spine   Thoracic spine

Sacrum

Mandible

Pelvis

Tail
bone

Scapula

Femur

Humerus

Kneecap

Elbow

Rib

Fibula

Radius

Sternum

Stifle
(knee)

Ulna

Tibia

Wrist (carpus)

Ankle
(hock)

Bones
of the
foot

Orbit

Nasal bone

Maxilla

Hinge joint

Upper mandible

Lower mandible
(vertical section)

Mandible

The skeleton is the framework for the body. All the dog's ligaments, muscles, and tendons are attached to the bones, 319 of them in total. By a process called ossification, cartilage template is calcified to produce bone. Bones are living tissue and they respond to the stresses and strains placed upon them. To build and keep healthy bones, dogs need a nutritionally balanced diet that contains an adequate supply of calcium, vitamin D, and phosphorus.

FIRST AID AND EMERGENCIES

The main aim of first aid is to provide emergency care and treatment of a sick or injured animal before full veterinary treatment can be arranged. Genuine emergencies include collapse, major injuries or bleeding, prolonged epileptic fits, severe diarrhea and vomiting blood, difficulty in breathing, prolonged whelping, burns, and poisoning. Some of these are covered below.

BLEEDING

◆ The escape of blood from a damaged blood vessel is called hemorrhage. Clean away any obvious dirt and apply a clean pressure dressing to protect the wound from further contamination and to slow the blood flow. A sterile non-adherent dressing, such as melanin, some cotton wool and a new conforming bandage, is ideal, but, failing that, improvise with a clean handkerchief and a long strip of cloth. If blood soaks through the first

layer, apply another on top—don't keep opening it up to check!

BROKEN BONES (FRACTURES)

◆ Bone fractures are always painful, but it can be very difficult to assess their severity at home. All cases of sudden onset lameness, especially after an obvious accident, should be examined

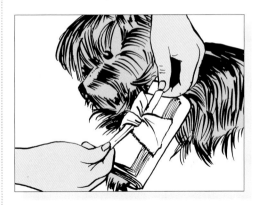

promptly by your vet, so call immediately for advice. Small cracks in young bones (greenstick fractures) may need no more than a support dressing and a couple of weeks of strict rest, whereas a major fracture involving a joint and with skin and muscle injuries may threaten the dog's ability to use the leg again.

◆ If your dog can walk on the other three legs, and there is no serious bleeding, it is generally better to restrict movement rather than try to apply dressings and carry him. If he cannot walk, this may be due to shock, multiple fractures or a back (spinal) injury, so improvise a stretcher (see page 123).

◆ Where the injury is in the lower leg, and there is a lot of movement and pain, keep your dog still by reassuring him until you can see the veterinarian. Generally, dressings do not help much and half-applied dressings that slip down may make matters worse.

◆ The only time when it is important to apply a dressing is when there is an open wound (see Bleeding, page 117 and Wounds, page 126).

BURNS

◆ Burns occur when the body tissues are damaged by heat, chemicals, electricity (including lightning), or radiation (e.g., sunburn). With electrical injuries, always turn off the supply at the main switch. Where the outer layer of skin is lost, there may be extensive fluid loss and infection. Burns need to be cleaned and kept sterile with regular dressings and antibiotics. Burns from house fires tend to be complicated by smoke damage to lungs and eyes. Use cold water to reduce the temperature of simple burns.

CHOKING

◆ Many dogs love playing with balls and other small objects that they can carry in their mouths, but it is best not to provide

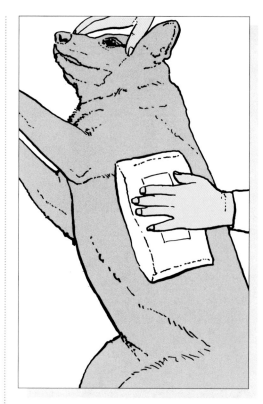

any that are small enough to go into the dog's throat. A ball half swallowed by mistake can block the passage of air and instantly cause a life-threatening choke.

◆ If this happens, move fast—your dog cannot breathe. If you cannot restrain your dog and reach the obstruction with a pair of pliers or tongs, try short, sharp, hard pushes to the abdomen, upward and forward, just below the rib cage (called the Heimlich maneuver in people). This is more likely to be effective than trying to dislodge the object from the throat with your fingers.

THE ABC OF FIRST AID

The golden **ABC** for a collapsed animal is:

◆ **Airway**—Is there anything blocking the airway through the mouth or throat, such as food or vomit, a ball or a bone? Be very careful if you have to put your fingers into the mouth: It is far better to use a piece of wood between the teeth to hold the mouth open than risk being bitten by a dog who is not fully aware of what he is doing.

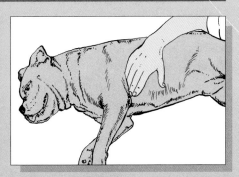

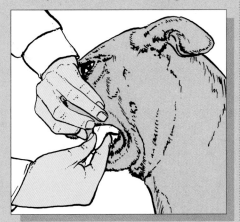

◆ **Breathing**—Is the animal's chest rising and falling? The normal breathing rate for a dog is between ten and thirty breaths per minute, or one every two to six seconds. If he is not breathing, gently compress the broadest part of the chest once every two seconds. Alternatively, holding the mouth closed, breathe into the nostrils to inflate the lungs repeating every two to three seconds.

◆ **Circulation**—Can you feel a heartbeat? Feel or listen to the side of the chest just behind the left elbow. A normal pulse rate for a dog is between 70 and 150 beats per minute, or one to two beats per second. If there is no heartbeat, try cardiac massage: With the dog on his side, firmly squeeze the lower part of the chest just behind the elbows, once a second. Every fourth beat, gently compress the whole chest wall.

Note: Call your veterinarian, and go straight to the veterinary clinic.

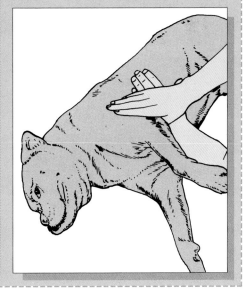

COLLAPSE

◆ A dog collapses when he is either suddenly or gradually unable to stand or coordinate his movements. It may be due to a wide range of causes, such as severe heart disease, serious injury, choke, internal bleeding, a metabolic problem, heatstroke, acute back pain, fits or poisoning. Treat as an emergency; contact your veterinarian.

CONVULSIONS (FITS)

◆ A dog may be having a fit if there are muscle tremors and twitching or violent muscle spasms. These may be accompanied by frothing at the mouth and the passing of urine and feces. The fit may be caused by epilepsy, poisoning, a metabolic disorder (e.g., low blood levels of glucose or calcium), infection, or injury to the nervous system.

◆ A classic epileptic fit will last just two to three minutes, although at the time this may seem much longer. It is not in itself an emergency. Your dog is best left well alone: clear away any fragile items or electrical cables, dim the lights, and keep the noise levels down. It is rare for a dog to swallow his tongue, so keep your fingers away from his mouth to avoid being bitten. As the convulsions subside, the dog will regain consciousness, although he may seem dazed and confused for awhile afterward. Arrange for him to have a full veterinary checkup.

Note: If the dog does not come out of the fit in a few minutes, you should contact your veterinarian and arrange to take him to the clinic immediately.

DIARRHEA

◆ A dog who is vomiting and is passing quantities of blood-stained diarrhea has hemorrhagic gastroenteritis. This may be caused by a virus, such as parvovirus, or one of a number of bacterial infections. He may rapidly become dehydrated and may go into shock from fluid loss.

◆ Do not give anything further by mouth, and seek veterinary help as soon as possible, as your dog may need to go on an intravenous drip to save his life.

◆ Simple diarrhea without vomiting is best managed at home by going without food for 24 hours, and offering plenty of clean water to drink.

◆ Severe diarrhea cases should receive veterinary care and will be better helped by drinking either a veterinary or children's oral rehydration fluid (available from a pharmacy).

DISLOCATION

◆ A displacement of a bone from its proper position in a joint is called a dislocation. Unless there is a congenital deformity, a dislocation will only occur in those instances when there has been significant trauma.

◆ Common sites in the dog are the hip and the elbow. They are associated with loss of movement, pain, and swelling.

Dislocations are better left without dressings. These injuries should be seen quickly: The faster they are replaced, the better the end result.

DROWNING
◆ Inhalation of water into the lungs, normally while swimming, may lead to your dog being unable to breathe and losing consciousness.
◆ Hold the dog up by his hind legs to clear excess fluid from the lungs and perform the resuscitation technique (see Collapse, page 120).

ELECTROCUTION
◆ The passage of electric current through the body may cause signs from mild irritation to unconsciousness and cardiac arrest.
◆ For the latter, perform the resuscitation procedure (see Collapse, page 120) but always turn the electricity supply off at the main switch first. Lightning strike is often accompanied by burns at the point of contact with the ground, pulmonary edema, and paralysis. Chewing at electrical wires will cause burns to the mouth and lips.

EYE PROLAPSE
◆ A major injury to the head after, for example, a road traffic accident, may cause the eyeball to be forced out of the socket.
◆ Try to prevent the eye from becoming soiled with dirt or hair, and take your dog immediately to the veterinarian. These eyes rarely function properly again, but if replaced quickly, look reasonable.

FOREIGN BODY
◆ Any foreign material that causes a problem is termed a foreign body.
TYPICALLY THESE ARE:
◆ **Grass seeds in ears:** These are very irritating, with persistent head shaking and scratching. Your veterinarian must remove them, possibly under anesthesia.
◆ **Grass seeds in eyes:** Discharge, pain, squinting, swelling. Check with the veterinarian.
◆ **Grass seeds in the foot:** Typically in mid-summer, affecting dogs with longer hair around their feet. Swelling and pain occur between the toes, forming an abscess. When this bursts, the seed may come out with the pus, or may need to be removed by your veterinarian. Bathe the foot three times daily with warm salt water.
◆ **Wood splinter or grit in the eye:** Copious rinsing with clean water may be enough to clear it, but foreign matter may be hidden behind the third eyelid, or embedded in the cornea. If pain persists, seek veterinary help.
◆ **Balls, bones, stones, small toys, and lengths of string in the gut:** When inadvertently swallowed, they may cause an obstruction of the intestine, causing persistent vomiting, pain, and depression. Seek veterinary help.

◆ **Wood, bone, or plant material in the mouth:** These items may become wedged between the teeth, causing distress and discomfort for the dog and, if left, local infection.

◆ **Dogs that have sticks thrown for them to chase,** do occasionally run onto them, causing deep wounds to the chest or back of the mouth. The main piece of wood may be easily removed, but splinters may remain in the wound, causing infection.

BLOAT OR GASTRIC DILATION/TORSION

◆ **Bloat** means that the dog's stomach becomes inflated with air and then twists on its attachments within the abdomen, with disastrous consequences. It is one of the few genuine emergencies. Luckily, it is relatively rare, and typically affects larger, deep-chested dogs.

◆ A dog developing this problem will show sudden onset of restlessness, dribbling of saliva, retching, pain, and sometimes extreme swelling of the abdomen. This may rapidly deteriorate to shock and collapse, and needs very urgent veterinary attention to release the buildup of gas, and restore normal blood circulation to the whole body.

HEART DISEASE

See the previous section (Heart and Circulation Diseases, page 107).

HEATSTROKE

◆ Dogs have thick fur coats on all the time, and can only cool off by panting and finding a cool corner or cold floor to lie on. Where the ambient temperature is high, such as in a hot car or on a very warm day, their cooling mechanisms may not be able to cope, and then their body temperature can start to rise, often with disastrous consequences. Dogs with heatstroke will be in great distress, panting heavily; their rectal temperature may rise to over 106°F (41°C), progressing through collapse to coma and death.

◆ They need cooling down rapidly: Use buckets of cold water or a hose, and transport the dog to the veterinary clinic if response is not rapid.

◆ Prevention is better and easier than cure: Never leave your dog in a car on a day when the temperature is over 65°F (18°C).

INJURY

◆ The common serious injuries for dogs are road traffic accidents: These may vary from no more than a bump and a fright to serious multiple trauma.

◆ Is your dog conscious? Check your ABC (see page 119). Is he bleeding? Can he walk? Is he getting better or worse?

◆ If he panics, gently restrain him—don't get bitten—and put on his collar and lead. Use a belt if nothing else is available.

◆ If he cannot walk it is best to keep him immobile until the veterinarian can

TEMPORARY MUZZLE

A temporary muzzle will allow a nervous, distressed or injured dog to be examined safely, without the risk of being bitten. A tape or bandage is secured around the muzzle as illustrated. However, a muzzle should not be applied in the following circumstances:

- Airway obstruction
- Loss of consciousness
- Compromised breathing or severe chest injury

1. Tie a knot in the bandage.
2. Wrap around the dog's muzzle with the knot under the lower jaw and tie on top of the muzzle.
3. Cross the ends under the jaw and tie firmly behind the dog's head.

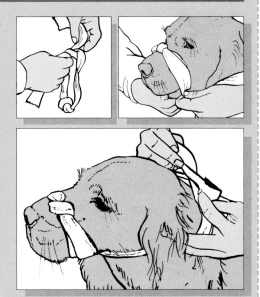

attend. If you need to move him, put a muzzle on him, improvise a stretcher with planks of wood, an old door, or a blanket, and slide rather than lift him onto it. If he has injured his back, moving him very carefully may make the difference between walking again and permanent paralysis.

◆ Don't offer anything to eat or drink until your pet has been examined by the veterinarian.

MILK FEVER

◆ Bitches producing large quantities of milk to feed a litter of puppies may run short of calcium in their circulating blood, with serious consequences.

◆ The signs include hypersensitivity, tremors and twitching. Urgent treatment with intravenous calcium is essential.

PAIN

◆ Pain in dogs is usually associated with skeletal injury or trauma, back problems, cancers, abdominal disease, such as pancreatitis or peritonitis, or the passage of urinary stones.

◆ Sudden onset of acute pain, with yelping or whimpering and reluctance to move, may be due to back pain, e.g., from a prolapsed intervertebral disk. Strict confinement of the dog is the best action until he has a full veterinary examination.

POISONING

◆ A poison is anything that, when eaten, breathed in, or absorbed through the skin, causes damage to the animal. Signs of poisoning are very variable, depending on the substance involved. The general advice given to dog owners is to:

◆ Prevent any further intake of poison.

COMMON POISONS

◆ **Antifreeze:** Dogs like the taste, but it can cause convulsions, coma, and death. Immediately contact the NAPCC at 1-800-548-2423.

◆ **Overdose with parasite (flea or tick) treatment:** This is the result of overenthusiastic owner dosing, causing twitching, salivating, and frequent urination. If from external treatments, wash the coat and seek veterinary help.

◆ **Rat or mouse bait:** Either dogs like the taste, or they may have eaten a poisioned rodent. Induce vomiting and take your dog to the veterinarian.

◆ **Slug bait:** Dogs like the taste. This can cause twitching, salivation, convulsions, and coma. You should induce vomiting and go to the veterinarian if any signs develop.

◆ **Chemicals:** Spillages and accidents. Wash any traces from the skin and then contact your veterinarian.

◆ **Prescription drugs:** Contact your veterinarian immediately.

◆ **Illegal drugs:** Contact your veterinarian.

◆ Keep a sample of the poison or the packet to show the veterinarian.

◆ As a rule, it is best to immediately consult with an expert if you think that your dog has been poisoned. You should telephone your veterinarian or the National Animal Poison Control Center (NAPCC) at 1-800-548-2423. You need to obtain expert advice on whether to induce vomiting, and how to properly do so—vomiting may cause damage to the lining of the dog's throat.

◆ Keep a sample of the vomit for analysis if necessary.

◆ Poisons on the coat should be washed off with a mild shampoo and then rinsed thoroughly with water.

SHOCK

◆ Shock is a very specific medical term for when there is sudden circulatory failure, due either to a major loss of blood or loss of the body's control over the heart and circulation.

◆ The signs of shock are weakness or

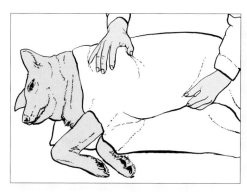

WHELPING

◆ **Pregnancy** in dogs lasts from 57 to 72 days (an average of 63 days). Whelping is the process of the bitch giving birth to a litter of puppies; it happens in three stages.

◆ **Stage 1** is the start of the rhythmical contractions of the womb, normally lasting six to twelve hours.

◆ **Stage 2** involves the rhythmical contractions of the abdomen. It leads to the breaking of the water, and results in the birth of puppies. The delay between each puppy is variable: from five minutes to several hours, but if it is more than one hour, then you should call your veterinarian for advice.

◆ **Stage 3** occurs when the bitch passes the afterbirth (placenta). It is common and normal for her to eat the placenta. In most mixed breeds whelping is trouble-free.

◆ **Dystocia** means that she is unable to pass the pups normally, either because they are too big (large father/small mother), because of a previous injury to the bitch's pelvis, or because her metabolism will not let her go into the second stage of labor, e.g., lack of calcium in the blood. A true dystocia may mean that a cesarean will be necessary to deliver the pups.

collapse, pale lips and gums (mucus membranes), cold skin, and a fast heart rate.

◆ Make sure your dog can breathe easily and cover him with a blanket to keep him warm. An animal in shock must be seen by a veterinarian as soon as possible.

SNAKEBITES

◆ Two small puncture wounds on a lower limb, in summertime, in an area known for the presence of snakes should make you suspicious of a snakebite. Treatment is aimed at limiting the spread of venom until a suitable serum can be administered.

◆ Use ice packs and tight bandages, and stop your dog from running around until you contact your veterinarian. Tourniquets should only be applied where there is expert knowledge as they can cause a lot of damage. Call your veterinarian for advice.

STINGS

◆ The common stings are from bees and wasps. These rarely need treatment, but

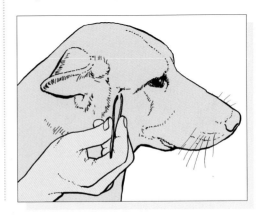

if causing much distress they can be soothed with cold water bathing or the use of an antihistamine cream.

◆ Try to remove a bee sting with some tweezers, but this may empty the rest of the bee venom into the wound, making things worse! If there is swelling around the mouth or throat, call your veterinarian.

◆ Some types of toad have toxins in their skin that can cause severe irritation, salivation, and swelling to the mouth if picked up. Rinse the mouth well.

THIRST

◆ If you suspect that your dog has an increased thirst, measure the amount he drinks each day. Anything over 3½ oz (100 ml) per 2.2 lb. (1 kg) body weight is abnormal and needs investigating. Causes include diet, sugar diabetes, kidney and liver problems, pyometra, hormonal abnormalities, pain, and fever. Call your veterinarian.

VAGINAL DISCHARGE

◆ Discharge may be due to a local vaginal infection or a pyometra. Consult your veterinarian.

VOMITING

◆ Dogs vomit very easily. It protects them from the possible consequences of a fairly nonselective appetite, but repeated regular vomiting is abnormal.

◆ Withhold all food and water by mouth until the vomiting has stopped, then offer small amounts of water regularly. If the vomiting is persistent, seek veterinary help (see Diarrhea, page 120).

WOUNDS

◆ **Large open wounds** need urgent veterinary attention. The main first aid objectives are to:

1. Prevent further injury
2. Prevent contamination of the wound with dirt
3. Control any bleeding

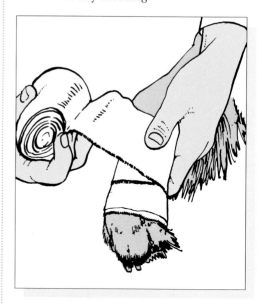

◆ **Bite wounds** may be contaminated with bacteria from another dog's teeth, so they need cleaning up as much as possible. Clip the hair from the wound edges, and wash freely with clean water. Antibiotic treatment should be started quickly to limit any wound infection.

INDEX

USEFUL ADDRESSES

American Society for the Prevention of Cruelty to Animals
424 East 92nd Street
New York, NY 10128

American Mixed Breed Obedience Registration
205 First Street
New Prague, MN 56071

National Animal Poison Control Center
1717 South Philo Road
Suite 36
Urbana, IL 61802

Delta Society
P.O. Box 1080
Renton, WA 98057-9906

American Humane Association
63 Inverness Drive East
Englewood, CO 80112

National Animal Control Association
P.O. Box 480851
Kansas City, MO 64118-0851

Humane Society of the United States
2100 L Street, NW
Washington, DC 20037